THE PROPHET
One Nation Under God, In All Her Wickedness

MELVIN E BARNETT

Melvin Barnett / Gateswood Press

www.melvinbarnett.com

ISBN: 978-0615529295

CONTENTS

ACKNOWLEDGMENTS

Most importantly I would like to thank those who have prayed and supported this ministry over the past years. Thanks to my wife, family, and close friends who have been a personal encouragement throughout years of ministry.

INTRODUCTION

What you are about to witness is a hypothetical situation between God, a Prophet, and a prophetic message to this nation. The message deals with the spiritual condition of the church and the nation at large. This is not just any book, written in any style; it is written in a manner that will captivate the mind and challenge the heart of every reader.

What kind of message would the prophet Jeremiah declare to the United States of America? If Isaiah said unto God, "Send me," what would the message be for today?

Without a doubt the Gospel is the most important message ever preached to the World. It is the message of the New Testament and the fulfillment of the Old. But what if, for the next few hours of your life, you could hear an Old Testament prophet declare the Word of God to this generation? Would you take time to put down what you are doing and listen to such a word? For the next few hours give mind to this novel and pray that God would use some part of this book to encourage you in your faith.

The content of this book and its prophetic layout will hopefully encourage you in your faith like that of any good book dealing with Christian issues. However, clarification of a few facts must be stated. Though issues found herein may directly relate, and support, that of many Christians, it is very important that ALL doctrine be based solely upon the Word of God. It is paramount to any Christian to respect and preserve the integrity of the written Word of God. That is why this book was written with great and prayerful caution.

The highest regards and respect for the Word of God is practiced, and preached, by the author of this novel. There is but one written Word of God, and that is the Holy Bible.

Melvin E. Barnett

1 THE BEGINNING OF THE END

Now the words of the Prophet are declared to this generation two millennia after the resurrection of the Lord Jesus Christ. And it came to pass that during the Dark Ages the Lord began to seek out one that would deliver the children of God into a country never known of or dwelt in by civilized man-- a country that would be built upon the Word of God, offering liberty from persecution of the saints. In those days there was much heresy and persecution of the saints, so that even the blood of many filled the streets as they were tortured and burned to death for their faith.

The cries of the saints were noised in heaven, and the Lord said, "Now I will deliver My children into a far country, that they might build great cities and multiply like the stars of the sky and the sands of the sea. There I will bless them that they may bless others; and they shall wax strong and exceed in number; their harvest shall go forth over all the earth. I will be with them in peace and in war. I will deliver their enemies into their hands, for they shall be My people, and they shall send the Gospel to the ends of the earth."

And in that day one man journeyed to a far country unknown by the world, and the Lord was with him. Soon God brought His servant to a new land that flowed with milk and honey. A land that was rich with gold and precious stones. Soon man began to multiply and wax strong in this distant land. God blessed the land and all its inhabitancy, for many were written in the Lamb's Book of Life. And the church began to grow and wax strong, and there was found peace throughout much of the land.

Many generations would be raised up by the Lord to unite the government of this land to one common bond and secure the religious freedom of all. The Word of God was proclaimed as the foundation for the government, and all its laws were in accordance with the Holy Scripture. In that day God raised up many men that would bring the nation together for the common good of all its inhabitance, and there they would write into Law the Word of God. In that day did the Lord impart wisdom and knowledge for men to understand the principles for a Godly foundation in this new nation, and all that was written abideth in truth even to this day.

The Lord blessed the land, and many people throughout all the earth made their way to this country to secure freedom, even to this day. For the Lord gave rest to many, and His Word was proclaimed throughout all the land, and the Church grew strong. Many peoples throughout the world found peace, and they made her their nation, and they were proud. Many saints escaped persecution to find a new life where men and women could freely worship.

Then the devil began to devise ways to destroy the land and corrupt the minds of its inhabitants, turning brother against brother and sister against sister till man fought over their own freedom. There were other reasons for this war, but Satan was defeated and God began to set men free, that they too could worship and enjoy the peace of God among all men. The Lord harkened unto the prayers of the saints, and soon the nation was reunited. From that time on great advances were made toward civilizing and industrializing the whole country. This nation rose in power and was a testament for the Lord Jesus Christ to the whole world.

Soon the whole country was settled and throughout the land the Lord continued to bless His children. In this day was the Word of God read throughout many houses, both of the rich and poor. Many believed upon the Lord Jesus Christ, and His teachings were taught unto many and for many generations. The next generations were hard, but God blessed His seed, and though the day required much work, at night, the ways of the Lord such as was commanded to all Israel were taught in many homes.

Knowledge grew throughout the whole earth and soon the inventions of man became very great. Industries began to flourish and each man labored according to his hire. Great cities began to be built throughout all the land. The means by which man traveled changed in these years; he no longer traveled by foot or animal, but by train, by ship, by automobile, and even by air. Cities were united by phone and man would send and receive messages at the same time.

Then there arose a great war among many nations. Nations allied with others, the whole world was divided, and there was war for many years. Cities laid in ruin as man swept through killing every man, woman, and child and leaving behind only ashes. Armies roamed the earth inside great beast-looking vessels full of fire and destruction. Such weapons of destruction had never been used in war until this hour. The saints prayed and God gave victory to His children for He was with them in all occasions. Soon after the great war every man returned home and continued in his way and there were many years of peace.

Despite the blessings of the Lord, Satan continually devised ways to bring man into bondage. As the days went by it was very obvious to the devil that he should begin to use some of the innovative ways of the world to come against Christians and to insure the decay of civilization. His tactics were well thought out as his demons carried out strategic plans to cause ruin throughout the World and see this nation crumble to her knees. What he didn't realize was the fact that God has always been in control, for the governments rest on His shoulders. Satan not only wanted to destroy the lives of Christians, but he hated this nation for her government as well, and he continually sought ways to destroy her.

Soon the devil began to strategically plan for what would become the downfall of this nation. He devised ways to enslave and indoctrinate the people of this land. His plans would take many decades to fulfill, but slowly he would have to lay the cornerstones of destruction. He knew that man was quick to worship material wealth, so he devised ways to compete with the ways of the Lord. The devil hated all human life, and because of his hate he would seek ways to destroy the unborn, the elderly, the unwanted, and the poor from off the earth. Slowly he would have to create what would seem to be good reasons for what would soon be total governmental control-- a one world government that would destroy all Christian doctrine -- one that he could ultimately, by the sovereignty of God, control.

Bringing down this nation would take many years, but she would have to crumble from the inside out. Satan would have to start immediately on a strategic initiative to see the whole world give in to his authority. The plan would start slowly and through decades or even centuries he would arrange for world events to occur. With each event, whether it be social, economic, or religious, each piece would be laid in place to build the beast that would take over the whole world and rule it. Not only would Satan plan for the demise of this blessed nation, but he would eventually plan for a global effort controlled by one government – a union of powerful nations aligned together with one purpose.

It would be important to raise up nations that would war against each other, to put into place political systems that force indoctrination, while other governments slowly rotted away in their own greediness. Militant governments would rise up to bring insecurity to the world, while others would spread their charm with diplomacy. Each nation would have their own character, while continually working to eventually crumble and give in to the desperate need of one government. Money would have to be used to finance all these initiatives and over centuries of time, Satan would have as his very own the purse strings of the world. Satan would finance two fighting nations, while holding the sovereignty of each nation at ransom.

With the whole world slowly developing economically an economic collapse would soon bring nations to their knees. In one day the value of money went to the bottom, causing many to take their own life. Satan thought if he could cause calamity in the earth many would curse God. However, in time of need, Christians turned to the Lord as their Provider. When times were tough, men and woman trusted the Lord for their next meal and God was there to provide and protect. During these days men and women worked hard to provide for their families. At night families spent time reading the Bible or doing other activities while exemplifying true values to their children. Sunday was a special time of rest, a time of family and gatherings, a time to put the hard week behind and rest for the one to come. Most of all, it was a time to be together in church.

Soon Satan knew that it was time to break up the family unit and to stop at nothing short. It was apparent that during hard times men and women pulled together and trusted in the Lord for their next meal. The unity of homes would have to be split up and homes would have to be torn apart through divorce, abuse, economic hardships, and false accusation in order to separate children from their parents.

While depression was imminent in this nation and across much of the world, Satan was once again trying to destroy the seed of Abraham as in times past. In the next few years there would be millions of Jews destroyed by the hands of wicked men. Controlled by demonic forces, men without a conscience would lead millions to their deaths. Wives and daughters would be raped and beaten in the streets. Children would have to watch as their parents were executed before their eyes. Men and women would be forced to undress and stand naked before their executioners; others would be gassed to death. Large ovens would be erected to burn the bodies, and pits dug to bury the remains. Some of the Jews were stripped and buried alive. Not only were the Jews being destroyed, but thousands of Christians were murdered as well during this time.

Then a war came like no one had ever seen before; the war of all wars. Three nations rose up against the world, and they fought for many years. During this time factories opened and the industries multiplied throughout all the land. During this war this nation would have to produce mass weapons and supplies for the war. For the first time many women had to go and work in the mills to supply the ever-growing war.

While husbands were away for war their wives worked diligently to supply the means to bring victory and see the war end. Day and night this nation did work to build ships and instruments of mass destruction. No longer were nights a time to rest, but became a time to work as well. In time many wives would lose their husbands in battle. Mothers would lose their sons. Children would lose their fathers.

This nation once again grew strong and great wealth returned to the land that flowed with milk and honey, but things would never be the same. After the war many wives and mothers continued in the work place. Women now labored along side men. Jobs that only men held now became filled by women as well. Slowly the family unit began to melt down and the morals of the country began to decrease with each new year. Much of the church remained content in its way instead of reaching out to the widow. Instead of reaching out to the fatherless children, they harbored to themselves and the government pulled the weight to relieve the burden.

Sadly, what would seem to be for the good of man, Satan would use in the future to destroy the family. This was one battle that Satan thought he had won. The devil's plan of creating a welfare state would soon unfold before this nation's eyes. He knew that it was vital to gain control over the homes and to enslave families to government programs and government entitlements. If he could ensure a welfare state it would give him opportunity to meddle in the lives of eventually every person in some way or another. This plan would be slow, but with the desire for material gain along with the now fast pace of society, he could pull it off in a few decades. Few would ever realize his work, and for those who did, they would be scorned by not only the heathen, but ones who professed Christ as well.

This nation grew strong and in no time her population began to multiply and God blessed His children and there was peace returned throughout most of the earth. The war was over and industries had to return back to supplying non-military materials and goods. Much of the earth was changed by the war and would never go back to its old ways. With war came expenses, and with expenses came loans. Soon many nations would find themselves in debt. This would eventually change this nation, and because of the greed of many, she would fall prey to the devil's plans. The government began to spend what it didn't have only to print more money to cover its debt. Soon the economic system would no longer be backed by gold, but rather by useless paper.

Debt continued to escalate, but many failed to see the handwriting on the walls. Mothers and fathers, now economically pressed to work, left their homes and their children so that they could provide for their family. Stress and pressure exploded, and caught up in their own lust, this nation soon began to part from the ways of the Lord. Children watched as their parents tore apart their homes, electing to go separate ways from the vows of marriage. Children were now in search of a mother that would train them up from a tender age, teaching them the ways of the Lord. Fathers in rebellion to the Lord forfeited their duty to be the priest of his house, refusing to exercise the dominion that God set in order from the beginning.

Soon women began to have to defend for themselves because men failed to be the man that God had made them to be. Selfishness and the cares of this world were soon to feed what would be the most hideous war against the home. With each day man would sink deeper into the wickedness of this world, denying all Godliness. One thing was for sure, through the unfolding of what Satan had planned, there remained the constant presence of the Lord, allowing all to take place. God was in control, not man nor devil.

For a final breakdown in civil responsibility, morality, and allegiance to the nation God had so blessed with great riches, war was to follow. Families would be split as young men and women would face leaving their home to go and fight in a distant land. By this time the economic system was very complex and the government had expanded to accommodate the needs of its people. But because of excessive debt and the increasing of government programs, this nation would continue to be suckered into a trap she would never be able to escape from. Strategically planning for each move, Satan orchestrated debt, family demise, moral decay, and perversion. Why? It enabled him to bring about what would soon be the epitome of a doomed civilization.

Now with the advent of television we began to entertain ourselves in the luxury of our own homes, sitting comfortably in front of the most wicked beast, one that would soon teach our children the ways of this world. Like a giant chess game, Satan played the pieces strategically against his opponent. There was only one catch, with each move of the devil, God's Word and prophecy became clearer to the discerning eye. His moves have often been prophesied for thousands of years, only revealing that there is a true God, a God that is ever ready to meet the needs of His people, a God that stands ready to forgive sinners and impart grace to them. You see, what the devil meant for harm, God has used it for good. The Word declares that His church will prevail.

With the passing of each decade, inventions and discoveries would take this nation to places never imagined by human minds. Medicine was being reinvented in what seemed like everyday. Communication was revolutionized. The knowledge of man was expanded each day as the whole world began to change. This nation would never be the same, and she would never return back to the simple lifestyles as before. Music now reflected the lifestyle of many that were separated from God. Words now reflected the ways of the world and all its sin.

War was imminent again. It was the youth that were barely out of school that surrendered their lives to fight for a cause that is still argued to this day, a war that many said was never won. As the young men and women were once again taken to a foreign land, many would never return home. For many, the enemy would never be known. Though the earth shook with the bombs built by man, the real enemy lurked in our own camps as well as our streets and cities. There would be no freedom won in this war, because freedom was sold in exchange for power and greed, sold for the price of thousands of young men and women. Politicians would dictate the war, seeking only to fulfill their own agenda of political gain and greed at the cost of soldiers. Our own nation, our own elected leaders, would sell us out.

Did the men and woman rebel against the government for sending them to war without a cause? Did parents question the leadership of their elected government? Yes, and many determined in their heart to rebel against a holy and righteous God; moreover, .their children cursed their parents and rebelled against all authority. Streets became places of protest for many. Hate and bigotry were at an all time high, and many wandered without direction as they turned themselves into living corpses with the use of illegal drugs. It was a time of rebellion for many. Children hated their parents and hated God as well. They rebelled against society and above all, the Lord. Society rebelled in their clothes, their lifestyle, and their music. An age of sexual freedom faced an ever increasing Godless society. People sought to defy the laws of God and commit hideous sexual sins in every manner imaginable. Unfortunately, the freedom that many thought they found, brought them into bondage with sexual transmitted diseases and moral corruption that turned into nails in the coffin of this nation.

The selfishness and sin of this generation would be passed down to the next. Defiance of the Word of God would only escalate in years to come. Children would hate their parents for not loving them, for not teaching them, and for not providing for them, and most of all, for not being there for them. Materialism would bring many families into debt, and therefore, put them into bondage for the rest of their lives. The children needed more than material wealth, but many would forget how to love and how to give from the heart. Because of the economic system, many mothers would now be forced into the work place. Because of the defiance of the Word of God, and lust of the flesh, many homes would be split and mothers and fathers would divorce, leaving their children to fend for themselves. What was home for the children would be turned into a battleground for selfishness, greed, lust, and anger.

With each phase of degeneration, certain characteristics of that era would come. Satan would now have to turn the minds of men and women to that of a child. Selfishness would escalate in marriage causing mothers and fathers to fight one another like children in the streets. Adults would play petty games, and each would avenge themselves, having no mercy on one another. Love would have to cease for the plan to unfold. It would be paramount for Satan to replace the true love that only comes from God to an unrealistic, selfish, sexual feeling. For the most part companionship between the man and woman would be defined in sexual terms instead of the desire first placed in the heart of each by the Living God.

To achieve this goal Satan would have to incorporate every possible means necessary. Slowly Satan would pollute the minds of mankind with immorality of every kind. Shame for ones sins would be accepted as normality. The knowledge and wisdom of the Word would have to be driven out from the schools and replaced with humanism -- the god of self.

With a society now out of control, our now corrupt government would come to the rescue, masquerading as caring about the welfare of society. The government would initiate programs to feed the poor, clothe the naked, shelter the homeless, educate the ignorant, convert the Godly, but much of its intentions would be laden with greed to control. The motives of government would be that of control, not help for the needy.

Satan knew that if he could create a welfare state it would give him a chance to indoctrinate a nation with apostasy and doctrines of demons. He knew that he would have to sell a package that looked good on the outside, but would destroy man on the inside. With an economic system out of control, education would mainly be left up to the state. Only now would the Federal government step in to control grants to the state, and with these grants there would be strings attached. Hideous programs would be created by the devil and carried out by the wicked to seek and indoctrinate nearly every possible child.

With mothers and fathers both working to just make ends meet, Satan could subtly sneak program after program into the public education without causing parental concern. With the use of special interest groups and media, he would launch a campaign to try and discredit any and all rejection to the programs. With the fast pace of society and family dysfunction, mothers and fathers would be sitting ducks. Children would be taught to report any measure of discipline to school officials. Slowly, the package would be unwrapped before the eyes of the whole world. With each step, nations would embrace the plan with open arms. Only the wise would be able to discern this work. Many Christians would be deceived along with the wicked.

Many children would become beguiled by hideous and demonic teachings. A whole generation of children being taken care of by the government would be taught that their parents are wrong and not fit to love them. Materialism would be the god of many. Satan would place programs in schools to rob the innocence of the children, teaching them the ways of Sodom and Gomorrah, and with a whole generation of parents without direction and discernment, Hollywood would take over at the end of the school day to finish the destruction that the government couldn't do during the day.

Murder would be a common act for every child to see. Sexual perversion would be masqueraded as wholesome behavior before every child, and with the perverseness of many parents, children would have no reason to believe otherwise. Power through witchcraft and other abominations would be introduced to children in schools, on television, and even in churches. Through the media and schools, children would be taught to seek every occasion to mock any Christian for their stand against the wiles of the devil, and to make fun of other children for their Godly upbringing at home. Their minds would be taught that Christians are hateful and should be persecuted for standing on the Word of God.

Of course there would always be those that would stand against evil, those that managed to train up the children in the ways of the Lord, but the earlier scenario would altogether fit most Americans lives. Sadly, many Christians would not even recognize the hand of the enemy. They would rather turn their back than to call sin, sin. Satan is alive and well, and for one that is judged already to be tormented in the pit, he would rather see nothing else but God's children corrupted, and the Gospel stopped from going forth. His hatred is so great against the human race that each year he destroys thousands of babies through abortion just to keep a person from having a chance to live and hear the gospel. But still, so many live each day fooled by the ways of the world. It is no wonder that God would send a prophet to proclaim his Word once again to this generation.

2 THE COMMAND

It was early one morning when the Lord spoke unto me concerning the condition of the church in America. The Lord said unto me, "I have called thee to be a prophet to this nation. Arise and go out into all the land proclaiming all that I shall show thee and tell thee. I will give thee many dreams in the months to come. Each dream will I interpret for you that ye may proclaim My Word to this wicked generation. I will give you instruction on what to prophesy to My people and what to prophesy to the wicked which refuse to hear My Word. For this cause will give thee power and grant life to complete all that I shall charge thee."

"I will protect thee and no harm shall come to thee, for man shall rise up against thee, but I will be with thee and shall fight for thee. I shall make thy message known unto all the nation, and whosoever shall receive thee shall I bless, and whosoever shall speak out against thee shall I strike dumb. Ye shall go into all the country proclaiming each message that I shall give thee, ministering to all, and bringing forth the Gospel to all men."

"From the beginning great men did set sail for this land to declare the Gospel to every creature and lo, a great silence has covered the church. Men have become afraid to declare the

Word in power. I have not changed My ways, neither have I softened My judgments against such a nation that would defile My statutes. This nation has sowed corrupt seed and shall in time reap corruptible things. Even now before the eyes of this nation hath the wicked been given power to control the government of this nation."

"I will anoint thee to speak forth and proclaim the Word of God to every man and woman of this nation. It is time for men to make decisions concerning their house. Too long hath the double-minded man played into the hands of the wicked. It is time for each man to decide where they shall stand according to the Word of God. I the Lord shall hang thee a plum-line, that every nation shall see their short coming. There shall be no middle ground for man to claim. For surely there cometh a season that the wicked shall seize the very powers of this world, and every man and woman shall have to know where they stand in the sight of God."

"The enemy has come to knowledge that shortly his time shall be no more, and he doth know that he shall be chained in the pit for eternity after the Judgment. My child, preach My Word with all thy heart, for great shall be thy reward. The Day of the Lord draweth nigh, and there is yet much work to be done. The wheat is ripe unto harvest. Still, there shall come a great revival and then a falling away. This nation shall reap the sin she has sowed, she shall be chastised for her great sins, but I will have mercy on My children. I shall not bring judgment upon My children, for there is judgment to come such that no man hath seen."

"Ye shall speak forth My Word, and I shall speak to thee concerning the sins of this world as ye go about to spread the Gospel. I shall fill thy mouth with My Word and hearts shall be changed, for I will be with thee throughout all your journey. My Spirit shall direct thee in all that ye shall say and do. I shall remind you of all things, and shall cause thee to speak forth boldly the Word of God."

"Arise My Child, go forth this day and proclaim the Word of God to all. I shall supply thy needs, and ye shall go forth and have all the necessities of life. I shall see that ye have food to eat and shelter at night. Ye shall be full, and thy strength will I increase that ye may be able to stand against the enemy. I shall go before thee and make a way for thee to do all that I have commanded this day."

3 MY WORD

Early one morning the Lord spoke and asked of me many questions. I said unto the Lord, "I am a simple man. Lord, I know not what thou asketh, nor do I understand thee." Then the Lord said unto me, "Why has thy people failed to believe My Word? Why have My people turned away from My Word to believe the words of man? Have I not done according to all that has been written? Will I find faith among My own children, for many fail to believe. Did I not instruct My people in all that they should preach, yet fables and lies do I hear from those that would lead My people. Where is the prophet? Where is the teacher? Why has the elder and the pastor been silenced? Has the apostle so soon become ashamed of all that I have promised?"

Then the Lord began to instruct me with a message to go and preach unto all the churches, "I received a message of repentance to declare to the children of the Living God." The Lord spoke to me many things concerning the church and its rebellion to the Gospel, even a deliberate assault on the children of God lead by the adversary himself, the devil. And I, the prophet of the Living God, do testify of the many things the Lord said unto me concerning the state of the church.

The Lord reminded me of the sayings of the children of Israel concerning Moses the servant of the Lord when God spoke from the burning bush saying, "I am the God of thy fathers, the God of Abraham, and the God of Isaac, and the God of Jacob." Then Moses trembled, and durst not behold. Then said the Lord to him, "Put off thy shoes from thy feet: for the place where thou standest is holy ground. I have seen the affliction of My people, which are in Egypt, and I have heard their groaning, and am come down to deliver them. And now come, I will send thee into Egypt."

This Moses whom they refuted saying, "Who made thee a ruler and a judge," the same did God send to be a ruler and a deliverer by the hand of the angel which appeared to him in the bush. He brought them out. After that he had showed wonders and signs in the land of Egypt, and in the Red Sea, and in the wilderness forty years. This is that Moses which said unto the children of Israel. "A Prophet shall the Lord your God raise up unto you of your brethren, like unto me; Him shall ye hear." This is he that was in the church in the wilderness with the angel which spake to him in Mount Sinai, and with our fathers: who received the lively oracles to give unto us: to whom our fathers would not obey, but thrust him from them, and in their hearts turned back again unto Egypt, saying unto Aaron, "Make us gods to go before us: for as for this Moses, which brought us out of the land of Egypt, we wot not what is become of him." And they made a calf in those days, and offered sacrifice unto the idol, and rejoiced in the works of their own hands.

From that time until now, the Lord has dealt with great patience with His children concerning their wickedness. From the Garden of Eden even to this evil generation that seeks all manner of wickedness against God hath He dealt with according to his laws. There is coming a time that man shall have no more time for repentance, a time that he shall be judged according to all his wickedness. How long shall man turn away from the Word of God? Even now has the Word of God come to me concerning

His Word, and the Lord spoke to me accordingly as I have written herein.

Then the Lord said, "My Word is eternal; all that I have inspired to be written is everlasting and shall stand against the fire. As it is written, 'Heaven and earth shall pass away, but My words shall not pass away.' Why do so many look to My Word with the understanding of a fool? Even from the beginning of time I have given men My Word and commanded them accordingly. All that I have spoken has come to pass in the day thereof, even in the days of Noah. I gave him My Word; and he built an ark that saved him and his children -- yet have I changed? Nay, I am the same today as I was in time past."

"When nations rose up against My people, I was with them. When they were persecuted and sold into slavery, I heard their prayers. My heart went out to My children as I heard their cry. So I chose a servant to lead them out of captivity, even one that would lead them into a land which flowed with milk and honey. At the appointed time My servant Moses rose up and went to Pharaoh to deliver My Word concerning the nation of Israel. Through the desert and the wilderness I protected My children. When they were hungered, I fed them. When they were athirst, I gave them drink. I was with them in the midst of the desert. In all that I promised, I, the Lord, delivered according to My Word. When they were confronted with the enemy, I gave them victory. Even the testimony of My power went out before them into all the nations. And many feared the hand of the Lord that was with Israel. All that I did was because of My love for mankind, for thou art created in My image."

"I showed mercy during times that I repented of even creating man. From the time man sinned against Me, My heart did yearn for that day he could be reconciled back to his created righteousness. Throughout time, I delivered and set a path for man to follow. In this path I covered and protected him from Satan. From the time I created man, even to this day, I have prepared a way for him to walk according to My righteousness.

Even in the midst of the sins of My children, I made a way for atonement and prepared a place in Abraham's bosom. Today I have prepared a way for My children to be forgiven of their sins. Christ, the Son of God, now stands at their heart's door. There is One that can cleanse the sins of this world -- even Jesus, the Christ, My only begotten Son".

"My little children, My Word has stood the test of time. Do not be deceived by the words of fools. All that I have said has come to past, yet many still require a sign to believe. Even in times of old, My people soon forgot all that I did in the wilderness. My people chose rather to study all the wickedness that they were delivered from and to worship heathen idols made from man's hands. They sacrificed their children in the fires of the gods. There women fornicated and committed great whordoms to serve their gods. It was not long after I delivered Israel from Egypt that My children soon forgot all the miracles I did. I commanded My children to teach their children the ways of the Lord and to tell them of the miracles wrought in the wilderness, but in time My children turned a deaf ear toward heaven and defied My commandments".

"I remember this day that I commanded My children concerning the commandments of the Lord. For it is written, 'And ye shall teach them your children, speaking of them when thou sittest in thine house, and when thou walkest by the way, when thou liest down, and when thou risest up. And thou shalt write them upon the doorposts of thine house, and upon thy gates: That your days may be multiplied, and the days of your children, in the land which the Lord sware unto your fathers to give them, as the days of heaven upon the earth. For if ye shall diligently keep all these commandments which I command you, to do them, to love the Lord your God, to walk in all His ways, and to cleave unto Him; then will the Lord drive out all these nations from before you, and ye shall possess greater nations and mightier than yourselves.'"

"Every place whereon the soles of your feet shall tread shall be yours: from the wilderness and Lebanon, from the river, the river Euphrates, even unto the uttermost sea shall your coast be. There shall no man be able to stand before you, for the Lord your God shall lay the fear of you and the dread of you upon all the land that ye shall tread upon, as I have said in time past, 'Behold, I set before you this day a blessing and a curse; a blessing, if ye obey the commandments of the Lord your God, which I command you this day; and a curse, if ye will not obey the commandments of the Lord your God, but turn aside out of the way which I command you this day, to go after other gods, which ye have not known.' How soon My children forgot all that I commanded and chose to put their faith in images of wood and stone, rather than the God of their fathers, even I AM."

"Where is the heathen? What righteousness does he bare? For I the Lord hath commanded thee in the ways of the wicked. For the curse of the Lord is in the house of the wicked, but he blesseth the habitation of the just. I say, enter not into the path of the wicked, and go not in the way of evil men, for the way of the wicked is as darkness, they know not at what they stumble. Know that the labor of the righteous tendeth to life, the fruit of the wicked to sin."

"My children hear My Words. The counsels of the wicked are deceit. The words of the wicked are to lie in wait for blood, but the mouth of the upright shall deliver them. He that saith unto the wicked, thou art righteous; him shall the people curse, nations shall abhor him. For I have given thee My Word, even My laws. Those that forsake the law praise the wicked, but such as keep the law contends with them. Know ye not that when the righteous are in authority, the people rejoice, but when the wicked beareth rule, the people mourn. For when the wicked are multiplied transgression increaseth, but the righteous shall see their fall."

"Know ye this day, My Word has come against the wicked. It is by My Word the craftiness of the transgressor is made known.

21

My Word doth instruct the wicked, as well as the righteous, yet how is it that My children have turned their ear from My voice? Just as I shall bring the wicked down low, I shall judge and bring the sins of My people to light. I, the Lord, shall not be deceived by the children of the devil; neither will I be mocked by My own. I am the Lord, and I am Holy."

"Did I not I command my servants, preach the word; be instant in season, out of season; reprove, rebuke, exhort with all long-suffering and doctrine. For the time will come when they will not endure sound doctrine; but after their own lusts shall they heap to themselves teachers, having itching ears; and they shall turn away their ears from the truth, and shall be turned unto fables. And lo, what I have written in time past is upon thee this hour".

"What servant would obey a fellow servant over that of his governor? What king would send his servant out into the field, only to have him heed the command of another? Would not the king's wrath be kindled against the servant's disobedience? What king would not require the life of that servant for his actions? For I am the Lord, I am a jealous God. I too shall require the obedience of my servants. Are kings and governors better than I? Can they number the hairs on thy head or count the sparrows that fall? I am the Lord thy God, and I am a jealous God. I shall have My vengeance in due time."

"I have surely called servants to preach, teach, and carry the Gospel to the corners of the earth, yet they have become fat at the tables of men. They are so quickly given over to the comforts of this world. They build great congregations -- then sit high and lifted up, seeking the praises of men like the Pharisees. Doth my Word not declare that pride goeth before destruction? I shall tear down and burn up what is made by hands. I, the Lord, shall see the destruction of the fruits of man's hands, even the fruit of his sweat, and I, the Lord, shall laugh in that day. I have commanded My servants to preach the Gospel, yet they slumber in the midst of their accusers."

"The time shall come that the wickedness of the hireling shall be manifest to the church. Their wickedness shall be exposed once and for all, for many shall point their finger and require an answer for their gospel. They shall say in that day, 'Why hast thou hid the truth from us? What manner of man would lie and steal from his own? What servant would lay comforted in his house, while the widow is without? What servant would pass the fatherless by to eat and drink in the houses of the rich?' Men shall say, 'Ye have robbed us of the truth and taught us according to thy own wickedness. Ye went before us teaching the ways of the Lord, but ye knew Him not, and deceived us by thy own word, and now we are judged ignorant of the truth.'"

"I, the Lord, doth declare that many have rejected My Word and created a false word that fulfills their own selfish, lustful desires. Many have added to My Word and hidden the truth. My Word is everlasting and shall be when all else is burned away. For many have set themselves up to be wise, thinking they shall fool many. They horde up riches and tend not unto the needy. These shall be cut off and divided up in the end. For I know my sheep, and they know my voice. Is it not written, 'Not every one that saith unto Me, "Lord, Lord," shall enter into the kingdom of heaven; but he that doeth the will of My Father which is in heaven?' Many will say to Me in that day, 'Lord, Lord, have we not prophesied in Thy name? and in Thy name have cast out devils? and in Thy name done many wonderful works?' And then will I profess unto them, 'I never knew you: depart from Me, ye that work iniquity.'"

"For there shall come a time when the Son of Man shall come in His glory, and all the holy angels with Him, then shall He sit upon the throne of His glory. And before Him shall be gathered all nations, and He shall separate them one from another, as a shepherd divideth his sheep from the goats; He shall set the sheep on His right hand, but the goats He shall place on the left. Then shall the King say unto them on His right hand, 'Come, ye blessed of My Father, inherit the kingdom prepared for you from the foundation of the world. For I was an hungered, and ye gave

Me meat. I was thirsty, and ye gave Me drink. I was a stranger, and ye took Me in. Naked, and ye clothed Me. I was sick, and ye visited Me. I was in prison, and ye came unto Me.'"

"Then shall the righteous answer Him, saying, 'Lord, when saw we Thee an hungered, and fed Thee? Thirsty, and gave Thee drink? When saw we Thee a stranger, and took Thee in, or naked, and clothed Thee? Or when saw we Thee sick, or in prison, and came unto Thee?' And the King shall answer and say unto them, 'Verily I say unto you, inasmuch as ye have done it unto one of the least of these My brethren, ye have done it unto Me.'"

"Then shall He say also unto them on the left hand, 'Depart from Me, ye cursed, into everlasting fire, prepared for the devil and his angels: For I was an hungered, and ye gave Me no meat: I was thirsty, and ye gave Me no drink: I was a stranger, and ye took Me not in: naked, and ye clothed Me not: sick, and in prison, and ye visited Me not.' Then shall they also answer Him, saying, 'Lord, when saw we Thee an hungered, or athirst, or a stranger, or naked, or sick, or in prison, and did not minister unto Thee?' Then shall He answer them, saying, 'Verily I say unto you, Inasmuch as ye did it not to one of the least of these, ye did it not to Me.' And these shall go away into everlasting punishment: but the righteous into life eternal."

"I see in this day men and women going about who proclaim to be religious. They make themselves to appear holy. They raise their voices to draw attention, and they make themselves appear to stand out from the rest. Loud and eloquent prayers they make before men. Who shall hear their prayers in the day of calamity? For their noise is fed into the roof as the limb is fed into the fire. In their hearts they think they know wisdom. They boast of great things, yet the needs of many go unmet. These men have defiled the Church in all their sins. Surely these servants of the Devil shall have their place with him - even in the fire of Hell."

"I have commanded, 'Thou shalt love the Lord thy God with all thy heart, and with all thy soul, and with all thy mind, and with all thy strength; this is the first commandment. And the second is like, namely this, thou shalt love thy neighbor as thyself. There is none other commandment greater than these.' My children are preserved unto life everlasting; they walk according to My Word. They shall humble themselves before Me, not boast of great things. Is it not written, 'The fear of the Lord is to hate evil: pride, and arrogancy, and the evil way, and the froward mouth, do I hate.'"

"Watch and pray that ye have discernment against thy enemy. For he doth hide in the midst of thee. Beware of false prophets which come to you in sheep's clothing, but inwardly they are ravening wolves; ye shall know them by their fruits. Do men gather grapes of thorns, or figs of thistles? Even so every good tree bringeth forth good fruit; but a corrupt tree bringeth forth evil fruit. A good tree cannot bring forth evil fruit, neither can a corrupt tree bring forth good fruit. Every tree that bringeth not forth good fruit is hewn down and cast into the fire. Wherefore by their fruits ye shall know them."

"Beware of those that offer you eternal life through your good works. They heed to themselves their self-righteousness. They draw men unto themselves, lifting themselves above many. Beware, My children, of false teachers that speak lies concerning My salvation. They are wise as the serpent, wanting nothing more than to bewitch thee. These are rebels of grace. They glory in themselves and their own righteous rather than the righteousness of the Son of Man. For their righteousness is as filthy rags. As it is written, 'There is none righteous, no, not one.'"

"Why are My children so soon beguiled by the words of false teachers? Have I not given thee My Word, and yet ye seek after your own righteousness rather than the righteousness of Christ. For they being ignorant of God's righteousness, and going about to establish their own righteousness, have not submitted themselves unto the righteousness of God. For Christ is the end of the law for righteousness to every one that believeth. For Moses describeth the righteousness which is of the law, that the man which doeth those things shall live by them. But the righteousness which is of faith speaketh on this wise, say not in thine heart, who shall ascend into heaven? (that is, to bring Christ down from above:) Or, who shall descend into the deep? (that is, to bring up Christ again from the dead.) But what saith it? The word is nigh thee, even in thy mouth, and in thy heart: that is, the word of faith, which we preach; that if thou shall confess with thy mouth the Lord Jesus, and shall believe in thine heart that God hath raised Him from the dead, thou shalt be saved. For with the heart man believeth unto righteousness; and with the mouth confession is made unto salvation."

"My child, salvation is simple, even unto the unlearned and ignorant. For My Word is wisdom and power forever. Lean not unto your own understanding, but believe that which is found in My Word. For My Word will quicken the dead, feed the hungry, and quench those that thirst. Receive not those that would bring railing accusations against Me and My Word, or even those that would stand and in My name tear down My Word. They shall be judged for their sin. For I am the Lord, and I desire to fellowship with thee this day. Soon ye shall enter in before My presence not many days hence. In that day shall ye enter in unto a mansion which is prepared for thee."

4 MY CHURCH

"Arise, write all that I shall tell thee down, that ye will know My Word. Then My child, see to it that thou understandeth all that I shall tell thee to write. For this day I have looked into the churches, and My heart is filled with sorrow for My people. How quickly men turn unto the fool, the infidel, and the heretic for their answers instead of unto Me. How quickly are they led down paths of destruction instead of harkening to My voice. They are so quickly fooled and bewitched by words of men when they go untaught by My word."

"Surely there is a time that shall come when men shall turn the Word into fables, and assault it before men. There is coming a time when once again Satan shall attempt to take the Word from My people. Those that have not learned and hidden My Word in their hearts shall be fooled by man, for I remember when man was without My written Word. They took pages and hid them, memorizing all that was written therein. In those days My people drew comfort from My Word, and My church grew despite persecution. Now, because of the hardness of man's heart, and despite all his accomplishments, he is once again returned to a place of ignorance regarding My Word. I tell thee a truth this day, with all the comforts and wisdom of this age, man is more ignorant of My Word than he has ever been since creation."

"In this age men will believe anything that seems mysterious, often putting meaning to it and attributing it to My work. Even now the churches need to be purged as in times past. Men and women need to stand for My Word. Lo, never have so many been so ignorant of My teachings, yet those that know My Word are counted among the fools. How has this come to be? For My Word is wisdom and life, not the babbling of a fool. Even now My servants are put down and scorned for standing on what is righteous. I see their despair, and in the end I shall avenge them, even I, the Lord."

"Once again My house, the church, is turned into a den of thieves. Men robbing and selling trash that needs to be put out and burned. Gold and silver are the gods of many. For My house is no longer a place of prayer and teaching, but a place of games and foolishness. My church has become like the merchant place, filled with crafts and such like items. Not only have My people failed to pay a tithe, but many masquerading as My servants steal the best that is brought into the storehouse."

"Go and prophesy unto the church saying, 'I the Lord have chosen My servants and lo, ye generation of vipers, ye thieves, ye sniff out the treasure and good of My people and bewitch them into giving to you what is Mine. Ye go before My people dressed in the finest garments, trimmed in fine jewelry, arrayed like the heathen without grace. For I am the God of My people, and shall I not take care of you? My children are not the children of the wicked peasant; they are not the children of a bastard. I give to My own good things. My children are a testimony of My goodness. I would not see their bodies naked before men. I prepare a place for My children to sleep. I prepare for them a table even before their enemies that they might eat and be filled. What glory shall I receive if the fool sayest to you, 'Canst your God feed you, can He not give thee shelter?'"

"My servant, even David the son of Jesse whom I anointed King of Israel hast said, 'I have been young, and now am old; yet have I not seen the righteous forsaken, nor his seed begging bread.' I the Lord art ever merciful, and lendeth; and My seed is blessed. Depart from evil, and do good; and dwell forevermore. For the Lord loveth judgment, and forsaketh not His saints; they are preserved forever: but the seed of the wicked shall be cut off. The righteous shall inherit the land, and dwell therein forever."

"And lo, so many seek only the riches of My people, plundering through all that My Children have, coveting the things of the world. Many go whoring after the image of the heathen, even before My people as they declare My Word. They are like the armies gathering spoil after the battle, seeking after My children, even playing on the heart of the widow and the old. I say unto them, lest they repent and turn away from their wickedness, they shall fall, and great shall be their fall."

"I have declared unto My people by My Word that I shall abide with them, and I shall protect them from their enemy. They need not hearken unto false prophets prophesying the words of Baal. They need not make sacrifices to man, nor do I require this day a sacrifice. I am God, and lo, I have justified My children through the final sacrifice of the Son of Man. Are ye wiser than I? Even I am God, and the Word hath created all that is made. For in God there are three, the Son hath His part, and the Holy Spirit hath His part, and the Father, even to Him, is there a part given and received in heaven. And many would come before Me making railing accusations. Who are they to tempt the Lord?"

"This world is the works of Mine hands, not the hand of men. I gave thee life, not another. Even the gods of the heathen are made out of My wood, My stone, and My gold and silver. Thou art a fool to believe that there is another God. As far as eye can see I have sowed the stars. As far as one can sail across the sea, I made each drop of water. For this is My earth, and My heaven, and I am God. I am a jealous God and I shall receive the confession of all men. For it is written, 'As I live,' saith the Lord, 'every knee shall bow to Me, and every tongue shall confess to God.' So then every man and woman shall give account of himself to God."

"Once again, My child, turn unto Me this day, repent and have faith, for I am God. Unto those that would rob from Me, I speak unto thee again the words of My prophet as said in times past and is come unto thee again. Thou art My own; thou art created in My likeness. I have given thee breath only to worship Me. I have given thee a mind to remember to praise me. If I have given to thee, why canst thou not return back unto Me what is Mine? Will a man rob God? Yet ye have robbed Me. But ye say, 'Wherein have we robbed Thee?' In tithes and offerings."

"Ye are cursed with a curse: for ye have robbed Me, even this whole nation. Bring ye all the tithes into the storehouse, that there may be meat in Mine house, and prove Me now herewith," saith the Lord of Hosts, "if I will not open you the windows of heaven, and pour you out a blessing, that there shall not be room enough to receive it. And I will rebuke the devourer for your sakes, and he shall not destroy the fruits of your ground; neither shall your vine cast her fruit before the time in the field," saith the Lord of hosts. "And all nations shall call you blessed: for ye shall be a delightsome land," saith the Lord of Hosts.

"Your words have been stout against Me," saith the Lord. "Yet ye say, 'what have we spoken so much against Thee?' Ye have said, 'It is vain to serve God: and what profit is it that we have kept His ordinance, and that we have walked mournfully before the Lord of Hosts? And now we call the proud happy; yea, they that work wickedness are set up; yea, they that tempt God are even delivered.' Then they that feared the Lord spake often one to another: and the Lord hearkened, and heard it, and a book of remembrance was written before Him for them that feared the Lord, and that thought upon His name. And they shall be Mine," saith the Lord of Hosts, "in that day when I make up My jewels; and I will spare them, as a man spareth his own son that serveth him. Then shall ye return, and discern between the righteous and the wicked, between him that serveth God and him that serveth Him not."

"For behold, the day cometh that shall burn as an oven; and all the proud, yea, and all that do wickedly shall be stubble: and the day that cometh shall burn them up," saith the Lord of Hosts, "that it shall leave them neither root nor branch. But unto you that fear My name shall the Son of Righteousness arise with healing in His wings; and ye shall go forth, and grow up as calves of the stall. And ye shall tread down the wicked; for they shall be ashes under the soles of your feet in the day that I shall do this," saith the Lord of hosts.

5 FIRST FRUITS

Again the Word of the Lord came to me concerning that which is set apart for the Lord, that which the Lord has claimed as His own but His children refuse to give up, that which is owed and declared sanctified by the Lord God. And the Lord did declare unto me all that I should go prophesy unto man. And according to the Word of the Lord I declare it unto all men, whether they be Jew or gentile, bond or free.

He that hath an ear, let him hear the prophecy of God, and to all that understandeth and abideth in this word, shalt they prosper in all that they set out to do. For God hath declared unto the church that they hath desecrated that which is His. That which is owed unto the Lord hath man said in his heart, "I will keep for myself because I regard not the Word of God nor do I claim My inheritance." For man hath become as the fool, lacking all wisdom concerning the things of God.

For in the beginning did God make heaven and earth, and on the seventh day He rested from all His work. And it was then that the Lord commanded man to observe that which He set apart and sanctified unto man. For it was man that needed to observe the Sabbath, not God. For the work of the Lord is forever and is continually purposed both day and night. God hath declared unto men, "Thou shalt have no other gods before Me. Thou shalt not make unto thee any graven image, or any likeness of any thing that is in heaven above, or that is in the earth beneath, or that is in the water under the earth: thou shalt not bow down thyself to them, nor serve them: for I the Lord thy God am a jealous God, visiting the iniquity of the fathers upon the children unto the third and fourth generation of them that hate Me; and showing mercy unto thousands of them that love Me, and keep My commandments. "

"Thou shalt not take the name of the Lord thy God in vain; for the Lord will not hold him guiltless that taketh His name in vain. Remember the Sabbath day, to keep it holy. Six days shalt thou labor, and do all thy work: but the seventh day is the Sabbath of the Lord thy God: in it thou shalt not do any work, thou, nor thy son, nor thy daughter, thy manservant, nor thy maidservant, nor thy cattle, nor thy stranger that is within thy gates: For in six days the Lord made heaven and earth, the sea, and all that is in them, and rested the seventh day: wherefore the Lord blessed the Sabbath day, and hallowed it.

But all that the Lord hath made Holy hath many trampled down before the Lord. In all that the Lord has required, many of His children hath kept for themselves. Yet in all things that come against them, doth they shake their hand toward heaven and curse God. But this day hath the Word come against them, declaring they have deceived themselves and been beguiled by the words of the devil. The thief cometh not, but for to steal, and to kill, and to destroy. In all that man shall do, the Lord hath declared Himself holy and to be first before all men. The Lord has declared His commandments unto man and hath set them in order to keep that which is His for the Day of Judgment. "

"Ye of little faith, why hast thou turned unto the words of man? Why hast thou forsaken the commandments of the Living God? For many shall say that God hath abolished that which was declared unto man before the resurrection, but that is the lie of the devil. For Christ hath fulfilled the law, but unto this generation hath He said, 'The first of all the commandments is, Hear, O Israel; The Lord our God is one Lord: And thou shalt love the Lord thy God with all thy heart, and with all thy soul, and with all thy mind, and with all thy strength: this is the first commandment. And the second is like, namely this, thou shalt love thy neighbor as thyself. There is none other commandment greater than these.'"

The Lord hath said, "If ye love Me, keep My commandments. And I will pray the Father, and He shall give you another Comforter, that He may abide with you forever; even the Spirit of Truth; whom the world cannot receive, because it seeth Him not, neither knoweth Him: but ye know Him; for He dwelleth with you, and shall be in you. I will not leave you comfortless: I will come to you. Yet a little while, and the world seeth Me no more; but ye see Me: because I live, ye shall live also. At that day ye shall know that I am in My Father, and ye in Me, and I in you. "

"He that hath My commandments and keepeth them, he it is that loveth Me: and he that loveth Me shall be loved of My Father, and I will love him, and will manifest Myself to him. Judas saith unto Him, not Iscariot, 'Lord, how is it that thou wilt manifest Thyself unto us, and not unto the world?' Jesus answered and said unto him, 'If a man loves Me, he will keep My Words: and My Father will love him, and We will come unto him, and make Our abode with him. He that loveth Me not keepeth not My sayings: and the Word which ye hear is not Mine, but the Father's which sent Me.'"

I declare to this nation, "It is come to pass that many hath rejected the Spirit of Truth for convenience's sake. For the Spirit of Truth reveals the Word of God and many hath turned their ear away from God's Word. For in it, they cannot live according to their flesh, but they are reproved before God. They hath said unto themselves, 'Yet a little while will I enjoy the things of this world and all its riches.' Hath they not read that by faith Moses, when he was come to years, refused to be called the son of Pharaoh's daughter; choosing rather to suffer affliction with the people of God, than to enjoy the pleasures of sin for a season; esteeming the reproach of Christ greater riches than the treasures in Egypt: for he had respect unto the recompense of the reward?"

"Ye children of the Living God, turn your eyes toward the heavens and seek after the righteousness of God. The Lord hath said, 'Therefore, take no thought, saying, "What shall we eat? or, what shall we drink? or, wherewithal shall we be clothed?" (For after all these things do the Gentiles seek:) for your Heavenly Father knoweth that ye have need of all these things. But seek ye first the Kingdom of God, and His righteousness; and all these things shall be added unto you. Is it in your power to add unto thyself anything? For thou canst even swear by thy head, because thou canst not make one hair white or black.'"

"The Lord knoweth the things thou art in need of and them shall He supply to His children. But many hath went about not trusting in the goodness of the mercies of God, but rather seeking after their own hearts' desire and not trusting in the Lord. Hath ye not read that the heart is deceitful above all things, and desperately wicked: who can know it? I, the Lord, search the heart; I try the reins, even to give every man according to his ways, and according to the fruit of his doings. As the partridge sitteth on eggs, and hatcheth them not; so he that getteth riches, and not by right, shall leave them in the midst of his days, and at his end shall be a fool."

"Hear the words of the Lord and obey. God hath required the first fruits of thine labor even as Abel brought forth the firstlings of the flock and sacrificed it before the Lord. Many of you hath done according to thy own will, saying thou hast done it for the Lord. Ye say unto men, 'I will give unto the Lord,' but your heart seeketh after wickedness. Your faith is in your own understanding, not the Word of God. For God hath declared unto this generation as He hath declared before, obedience is better than sacrifice. "

"I declare unto you this day, give that which is sanctified unto God. Ye have neglected the holy days. Ye work and toil until the day is far spent, seeking the riches of this world. Ye labor in vein, for the Lord giveth life and He taketh life. Thy labors shall become a stumbling block before thee and others. Why hast thou turned away from assembling thyself with the believer? Is fellowship with the heathen greater than that of thy Creator? What shall ye say when sickness hast come against thee?"

"What shall ye say when family hath turned against thee and forsaken thee? For even as the Lord did offer up His only begotten Son to die for thee, ye must offer up unto the Lord thy obedience. For on the first day was the Son of God resurrected for the sins of the world, so shalt that day be set aside to be remembered. For God hath given on the first unto man, so shall man return and offer back unto God. Sayest thou with an arrogant heart unto the Lord, 'Is there a day holier than the next?' Nay, thou hast hidden thyself from the Lord and refused to assemble with His children. Ye can not make boastful excuses of thy transgression before the Lord and thy neighbor. Know ye not that the eyes of the Lord are in every place, beholding the evil and the good?"

"For God commendeth His love toward us, in that, while we were yet sinners, Christ died for us. Much more then, being now justified by His blood, we shall be saved from wrath through Him. For if, when we were enemies, we were reconciled to God by the death of His Son, much more, being reconciled, we shall be saved by His life. And not only so, but we also joy in God through our Lord Jesus Christ, by Whom we have now received the atonement. Wherefore, as by one man sin entered into the world, and death by sin; and so death passed upon all men, for that all have sinned. Children of the Living God, Christ hath laid down His life that we can have atonement through His blood.

He hath reconciled us by His death and being saved by His life, yet many walk in ignorance of this truth."

"If ye, being reconciled by Christ Jesus and forever saved from hell, why canst thou walk not according to the statues of God? He has given thee life when thou wast condemned even to death and eternity in hell. He hath paid thy debt that ye could go free before God, being justified by the Blood of the Lamb. Hath ye forgotten that which the Lord hath done for thee? The wicked are cast out from before the Lord because of sins debt, yet ye, having been justified by faith, live and seek after the things of the wicked. "

"The wicked shall have their place in the fire which burns forever and ever, but ye were acquitted of thy offense before the Lord. Ye have been bought with a price. Thy name hath been recorded in the Lamb's Book of Life. Repent and turn from the ways of the wicked. Search out the wisdom of God this day, and turn from the way of the fool. Take heed to the Word of the Lord and let His Word quicken thee. In His Word shalt thy find refuge from this world. In His Word shalt thy find peace and contentment.

"The heathen hath sought to lay up treasures. By his works he hath said in his heart that he shall do well when old age hath come to past. For in his youth he regardeth not the things which are honest, but rather choosing to deceive his friend and lie before his master. Gold and silver hath he laid up for himself in his own house. He hath laid claim to wisdom and knowledge, choosing to ignore the commandments of the Lord. He hath hardened his heart against the Lord, choosing only to mock and blaspheme the name of the Lord, but in the Day of Judgment he shall cry out before God and man- who shall redeem his soul in that day?"

"In the Day of Judgment, shall the wicked pay a ransom to be set free? Shall his gold and silver pay his debt? For in his life hath he lied and cheated, seeking to gain wealth for himself. He hath spent his life enslaved to that which purchased material things on earth. The wicked man searcheth out that which is given freely of the Lord, but rather than submitting to the Lord, he hath spent his life trying to buy that which is free. Know ye this day that the gold of many shall cover the streets of Heaven. In that day shall every wicked man be judged and condemned before the throne of God, and in that time shall the wicked lay sight on every precious stone and substance he sold his soul to. The wicked hath searched his days for peace and fulfillment and knoweth not that which was free to all men in Christ Jesus. "

"His god shall betray him before his death. His god shall remain silent before him as the death angel comes to bind him and cast him into hell. All that he hath gained through his sweat shall be freely given to every saint. The gold that he sold his soul to shall pave the streets of Heaven, and there before the throne of God as it is written, 'As I live,' saith the Lord, 'every knee shall bow to Me, and every tongue shall confess to God.' So then every one of us shall give account of himself to God. And on that day, who shall write his name in the Lamb's Book of Life, for then it shall be too late."

"My children, thou hast become like many of the wicked, and ye shall be chastised for thy sins. For ye also have committed adultery with the god of this world. Ye too have went a whoring after the harlots of this world. Many of you hath joined thyself with harlots and desecrated the temple of thy body. The Spirit of God that is within, and hath sealed thee, hath ye openly shamed and grieved. Knowest ye not that the Lord is Holy, and all that is God, even the Son and the Spirit, are God in the same? Hath ye no regard for the Lord this day?"

"For the Lord Jesus Christ hath made a way for you to escape every temptation, and when ye are drawn away into sin, ye crucify to yourself the Son of God afresh, and put Him to an open shame. The Son of God hath paid the debt of sin once and for all, and it was that sacrifice that purchased your soul, and it is expedient that ye live separated from that which is sin. And likewise hath the Holy Spirit begun a new work in you that ye should know that which is sinful and that which is righteous. For the Spirit reveals that which is true, but many of you are stiff-necked like the seed of Abraham. "

"Ye care not that you are a stumbling block for the cause of Christ. Ye say in thine heart, 'I will work and gain that which I can and lay up for myself.' Ye labor day and night, never taking time to serve the Lord and assemble yourself with the saints. Ye even mock that which is holy and righteous. Thy discernment is become that of a fool, because thou hast turned away from the Word of God. Ye say to yourself, 'It is morning. I shall arise and go and make a wage for this day.' At night ye say to yourself, 'It is late, and I must rest now.' Why hast thou turned aside from the Lord? Thou art so quickly deceived by the ways of this world."

"Lay not up for yourselves treasures upon earth, where moth and rust doth corrupt, and where thieves break through and steal: but lay up for yourselves treasures in heaven, where neither moth nor rust doth corrupt, and where thieves do not break through nor steal: for where your treasure is, there will your heart be also. Repent and return back to the Word of the Living God. Give that which belongeth to the Lord back unto Him. My children, serve God with all your heart, with all your might, and say unto the wicked and the gods of this world, 'As for me and my house, we shall serve the Lord.'"

6 THE HARLOTRY OF GOD'S CHILDREN

Now the Word of the Lord came unto the Prophet concerning the harlotry of the children of God, because for generations she hath played the harlot before God. In times past hath the children of God went whoring after the gods of this world, forsaking the Lord and choosing rather to worship in the mountains, bowing down to graven images made by hands. Not only have they bowed themselves down to worship these idols, but many have sacrificed their children in the fire. Suddenly the words of the prophet Jeremiah filled my ears and I clearly understood all that the Lord said.

"They say, If a man put away his wife, and she go from him, and become another man's, shall he return unto her again? shall not that land be greatly polluted? but thou hast played the harlot with many lovers; yet return again to Me," saith the LORD. "Lift up thine eyes unto the high places, and see where thou hast polluted the land with thy whoredoms and with thy wickedness. Therefore the showers have been withholden, and there hath been no latter rain; and thou hadst a whore's forehead, thou refusest to be ashamed. Wilt thou not from this time cry unto Me, 'My Father, thou art the guide of My youth? Will He reserve

His anger forever? Will He keep it to the end?' Behold, thou hast spoken and done evil things as thou could. "

The Lord said also unto me, "As in the days of Josiah the king, hast thou seen that which backsliding Israel hath done? She is gone up upon every high mountain and under every green tree, and there hath played the harlot. And I said after she had done all these things, 'Turn thou unto Me,' but she returned not, and her treacherous sister Judah saw it. And I saw when for all the causes whereby backsliding Israel committed adultery I had put her away, and given her a bill of divorce; yet her treacherous sister Judah feared not, but went and played the harlot also."

"And it came to pass through the lightness of her whoredom, that she defiled the land, and committed adultery with stones and with stocks. And yet for all this her treacherous sister Judah hath not turned unto Me with her whole heart, but feignedly," saith the Lord. And the Lord said unto me, "Backsliding Israel hath justified herself more than treacherous Judah. Go and proclaim these words toward the north, and say, 'Return, thou backsliding Israel,' saith the Lord; 'and I will not cause Mine anger to fall upon you: for I am merciful,' saith the Lord, 'and I will not keep anger forever. Only acknowledge thine iniquity, that thou hast transgressed against the Lord thy God, and hast scattered thy ways to the strangers under every green tree, and ye have not obeyed My voice,' saith the Lord. 'Turn, O backsliding children,' saith the Lord; 'for I am married unto you: and I will take you one of a city, and two of a family, and I will bring you to Zion: And I will give you pastors according to Mine heart, which shall feed you with knowledge and understanding. '"

"And it shall come to pass, when ye be multiplied and increased in the land, in those days," saith the Lord, "they shall say no more, 'The ark of the covenant of the Lord:' neither shall it come to mind: neither shall they remember it; neither shall they visit it; neither shall that be done any more. At that time they shall call Jerusalem the throne of the Lord; and all the nations shall be gathered unto it, to the name of the Lord, to Jerusalem: neither shall they walk any more after the imagination of their evil heart. In those days the house of Judah shall walk with the house of Israel, and they shall come together out of the land of the north to the land that I have given for an inheritance unto your fathers. "

"But I said, "How shall I put thee among the children, and give thee a pleasant land, a goodly heritage of the hosts of nations?' and I said, 'Thou shalt call Me, My Father; and shalt not turn away from Me. Surely as a wife treacherously departeth from her husband, so have ye dealt treacherously with Me, O house of Israel,' saith the Lord. 'A voice was heard upon the high places, weeping and supplications of the children of Israel: for they have perverted their way, and they have forgotten the Lord their God.'" "Return, ye backsliding children, and I will heal your backslidings."

"Behold, we come unto thee; for thou art the Lord our God. Truly in vain is salvation hoped for from the hills, and from the multitude of mountains: truly in the Lord our God is the salvation of Israel. For shame hath devoured the labour of our fathers from our youth; their flocks and their herds, their sons and their daughters. We lie down in our shame, and our confusion covereth us: for we have sinned against the Lord our God, we and our fathers, from our youth even unto this day, and have not obeyed the voice of the Lord our God."

Now after the words of Jeremiah the prophet, the Lord God began to speak to me concerning this generation and the harlotries of the church. And as the Lord spoke these great things, a deep sleep overcame me and I remembered only the dream for a great while. Then after many days the words returned unto me and I understood all that I dreamed. For the Lord not only gave me the dream, but interpreted it not many days later, and behold now is the dream made manifest unto all nations, and before every man and woman.

Behold there appeared unto me a woman greatly adorned with the riches of this earth, her beauty was great to behold. And I looked, and she went as she pleased and all that were around her made way, for she was true unto her master. And in all the earth was her master made known, and all the earth feared because of his great strength. One day the master's wife decided to cast her eyes upon the things of this world, and she was filled with want for things around her. Then came her master saying unto her, woman come unto me and leave all that is before thee, for thou art mine own, and the things which thou hast seen art evil and shall cause thee to stumble. And the woman returned with her master but she kept all things she had seen unto herself.

On the next day, behold the woman went again unto the city and did marvel at all that she saw. For though her wealth was manifest unto all the world, she desired in her mind to be content with the apparel of those around her. Not realizing that she possessed all that every woman should hope and dream of, she desired to be like those about her. She desired the things of the world rather than the riches of her master. Then came her master again unto her saying, "Woman, all that thou hast set thine eye on is unclean and shall cause thee to stumble," and the master took again his wife and they returned again to their own house.

Soon, the wife, being headstrong, went again into the city and marveled with great lust for the things she was without. For she had pled with her master for the things which she saw outside her house, but her master said, "Nay, for all that thou desirest shall make thee unclean and shall be as rot in thine heart." She continually complained and sought after all that which was evil in the sight of her master. With each day she grew apart from her master seeking after the ways of the heathen and the lust thereof. Each passing day the love for her master grew weaker until she set in her mind that she would leave her master and not return home. For now she was willing to dwell in the midst of the heathen. So the woman departed from her master's house and did according to her own lust.

Now, seeing that the woman had left, the master sent servants to go and fetch his wife and bid her to return home. But after many days the servants returned unto the master saying, "For many days have we searched for thy wife and still we have not found her." After the servants of the master returned unto their post, the master was very sorrowful and did lament as though she was dead. The master loved his wife and gave her the desires of her heart, and all that was excellent she received from his hands. Each day the master's love for his wife grew and he would give all that he had to have her back again, but she hid herself from her master and chose to dwell in the tents of the wicked.

Soon, the wife had sold all that she possessed to buy food and shelter, and she said to herself, "I will arise and go unto my master, for I know that his love for me burns. I shall ask him to forgive me and have the servants of the house to prepare me a meal. Then shall I bathe and put on fine garments once again and I shall bid my master's forgiveness." So the wife returned again unto the master as she had planned. And when the woman was come nigh unto the master's house certain servants went and told their master, "Behold, thy wife whom thou seekest hath returned." And the master was filled with great joy and took her again and clothed her with fine garments and placed gold upon her neck and rings upon her fingers and she remained with him for a short while.

And again the wife said unto herself, "I will go again unto the tents of the wicked that I may once again do that which I desire." And she gathered her garments and fled from her master to a strange city. And there she did all that she pleased and remained content in her heart for a great time. And all that she did was evil in the sight of her master and she was soon found without. She again decided to return unto her master and find refuge and clean garments and fine jewelry to adorn herself with. So the woman returned again unto her master and he was filled with great joy for his love had returned unto him.

Then after a short while she again set her heart to return back unto the wickedness of the world and she left her master again. Then her master said unto himself "For this great wickedness I will give her a bill of divorce and she shall be free to do all that she pleases and she shall be free to go in and out of the tents of the wicked and dwell among the heathen, for now she had committed great whordoms in the streets." And lo, she was nowhere to be found and was even feared dead. Because of the love for his wife he did not put her away, but released her to be free.

And her face was known to many and she bore no shame for her sins. And again she returned unto the places of the wicked and she sacrificed unto every known god and worshipped in the mountains and in the vineyards. Every imaginable deed did she commit against the Lord. Even in the midst of her sin did her master love her and long to be with her again, but she remained, dwelling in the tents of the wicked, worshipping idols of wood and stone.

Soon, when all that she had was sold and she had no money, she dressed the part of the prostitute and sold herself to the wicked. For in her was no shame as she did all that her flesh desired before man. For her beauty was now scarred with the sickness of this world, and her countenance had fallen. She, having little strength in her bones, was now pushed about and counted with the beggars of the street. Everyone that once regarded her for her master's sake, now raped her openly in the streets, mocking her, and beating her openly outside the gates of the city. For now she had become sorrowful for all her sins and realized what she had done, but it was too late. The woman was taken as a slave to work in the heat of the day, only to be paid with a days ration and place to sleep.

The once beautiful woman was now covered by scars, dirt, and tears, and there she had no hope for tomorrow, only praying that her days on earth would draw nigh. For she had remembered all that her master did for her and how he loved her despite her sins. And the strength of the woman grew weak, and she was mocked through out all the land, for her beauty was fallen, and her virtue was scorned by all. Many shook their heads as they passed her by in the fields, only to be a slave the rest of her days

And the woman could now see that all she desired was evil, and all that she hoped to gain was laid to her defeat. The woman then said unto herself, "The life I lusted after has robbed me of all virtue and now I have nothing." Now the woman was very sorry for all her sins and she was ashamed. All that she had lusted after was a lie, and she knew that the wicked were slaves to their own misery, and the woman cried out, for she knew that all that she had done was evil in the sight of her master, and she was now filled with bitter sorrow as she sorely wept.

Then one day, while the master was in this great city to buy grain and trade with the merchants, he noticed that a crowd had gathered in the midst of the city to buy slaves for themselves. And being curious the master went out and drew nigh unto the crowd. Suddenly the master looked and behold, the woman he had loved for so many years was there before the multitude. And some of the people did laugh and mock her, for some remembered her greatness and now they rejoiced at her calamity, for they knew that her master was a just and righteous man before all and there was found no guile in him. And the master's heart was broken as he looked upon the woman stripped of nearly all her clothes and bound with chains.

Suddenly the crowd began to quiet as the master approached the auction block, and when the crowd had made way for the master, the woman raised her head and there before her eyes stood her master, and she then wept bitterly, for her shame was great, and the master took off his coat and placed it around her to cover her nakedness and kissed her. And the woman begged of her master for forgiveness and there he purchased her for fifteen pieces of silver, and for an homer and one half of barley. And the master said unto her, "Arise my love and return I pray thee with me this day." The master said unto the woman, "Thou shalt abide in my house. Ye shalt not play the harlot, and ye shalt not be for another man, and so will I also be for thee." And they twain returned unto their own city, and were joined again as husband and wife.

Now hath the Lord given me the interpretation of this dream to be declared unto his people. And I the prophet of the Lord do testify of all that the Lord hath shown me and spoken unto me this day before this land. For God hath seen the works of the wicked, and even now he awaits for the gathering of His children. For soon that time shall draw nigh, and nation shall gather with nation, and they shall prepare to war against Jerusalem. And all the earth shall turn against the saints and they shall be hated and despised for their faith. For the mystery of iniquity doth already work: only He who now letteth will let, until he be taken out of the way. And then shall that wicked be revealed, whom the Lord shall consume with the Spirit of His mouth, and shall destroy with the brightness of His coming: even him, whose coming is after the working of Satan with all power and signs and lying wonders, and with all deceivableness of unrighteousness in them that perish; because they received not the love of the truth, that they might be saved.

"He that hath ear let him hear this day. For God hath called His children unto repentance, that they make themselves ready, for the Kingdom of God is at hand. For since the beginning of time hath the children of God murmured and complained of all that hath been set before them by the Lord. For ye are stiffnecked and hath a hard heart. Ye have committed whordoms with the world around you. Ye have played the harlot before the Lord with every evil nation. Thou hast worshipped idols and brought them into thy house. Even this day have ye put strange images before the Lord and worshipped them. For the Lord seeth your iniquity and hath called you unto repentance. "

"This day the Lord hath commanded thee to choose whom ye will serve. Is it not written, 'No man can serve two masters: for either he will hate the one, and love the other; or else he will hold to the one, and despise the other. Ye cannot serve God and Mammon.' Therefore I say unto you, 'Take no thought for your life, what ye shall eat, or what ye shall drink; nor yet for your body, what ye shall put on. Is not the life more than meat, and the body than raiment? For the Lord shall provide all your needs if thou wilt turn unto Him this day. For the Just shall live by faith and this day hath the Lord called you to trust in Him. '"

"Because of thy greed ye have become a servant to the wicked. Ye hath sacrificed to the gods of this world and not turned unto the Lord your God. I say unto you this day, 'The Lord shall receive you this day if ye wilt turn from thy wickedness and obey His Word. He has purchased thee with a price, even with the blood of Jesus Christ. Ye are not your own, but I have paid the penalty for thy deeds. For once thou were in bondage unto the law and condemned before the Lord. Thy debt was to be paid with thy life, but many are backslidden, and now have ye been seduced by the lust of this world. Ye serve yourselves and deny that which is good, but I say unto thee, 'This day, if ye being free hath gained liberty, why hast thou been shackled and made a slave to this world?'"

"Know ye not that your body is the temple of the Holy Ghost which is in you, which ye have of God, and ye are not your own? For ye are bought with a price: therefore glorify God in your body, and in your spirit, which are God's. Forasmuch as ye know that ye were not redeemed with corruptible things, as silver and gold, from your vain conversation received by tradition from your fathers; but with the precious blood of Christ, as of a lamb without blemish and without spot: Who verily was foreordained before the foundation of the world, but was manifest in these last times for you, Who by him do believe in God, that raised Him up from the dead, and gave Him glory; that your faith and hope might be in God. Seeing ye have purified your souls in obeying the truth through the Spirit unto unfeigned love of the brethren, see that ye love one another with a pure heart fervently: being born again, not of corruptible seed, but of incorruptible, by the Word of God, which liveth and abideth for ever."

"For this day is the Lord your master, and ye are His children and He hath called you this day unto repentance. For the Lord your God is not slack concerning His promises. For soon the Kingdom of God shall be revealed unto all men. And many shall weep in that day, but in that day it shall be too late. For it is written, 'The Kingdom of Heaven is likened unto ten virgins, which took their lamps, and went forth to meet the bridegroom. And five of them were wise, and five were foolish. They that were foolish took their lamps, and took no oil with them, but the wise took oil in their vessels with their lamps. While the bridegroom tarried, they all slumbered and slept. And at midnight there was a cry made, "Behold, the bridegroom cometh; go ye out to meet him." Then all those virgins arose, and trimmed their lamps. And the foolish said unto the wise, "Give us of your oil; for our lamps are gone out." But the wise answered, saying, "Not so; lest there be not enough for us and you: but go ye rather to them that sell, and buy for yourselves." And while they went to buy, the bridegroom came; and they that were ready went in with him to the marriage: and the door was shut. Afterward came also the other virgins, saying, "Lord, Lord, open to us." But he answered and said, "Verily I say unto you, I know you not." Watch therefore, for ye know neither the day nor the hour wherein the Son of Man cometh. '"

"And again it is written, 'And He said unto the disciples, "The days will come, when ye shall desire to see one of the days of the Son of Man, and ye shall not see it. And they shall say to you, See here; or, see there: go not after them, nor follow them. For as the lightning, that lighteneth out of the one part under heaven, shineth unto the other part under heaven; so shall also the Son of Man be in His day. But first must He suffer many things, and be rejected of this generation. And as it was in the days of Noah, so shall it be also in the days of the Son of Man. They did eat, they drank, they married wives, they were given in marriage, until the day that Noah entered into the ark, and the flood came, and destroyed them all.

Likewise also as it was in the days of Lot; they did eat, they drank, they bought, they sold, they planted, they builded; but the same day that Lot went out of Sodom it rained fire and brimstone from heaven, and destroyed them all. Even thus shall it be in the day when the Son of Man is revealed. In that day, he which shall be upon the housetop, and his stuff in the house, let him not come down to take it away: and he that is in the field, let him likewise not return back. Remember Lot's wife. Whosoever shall seek to save his life shall lose it; and whosoever shall lose his life shall preserve it. I tell you, in that night there shall be two men in one bed; the one shall be taken, and the other shall be left. Two women shall be grinding together; the one shall be taken, and the other left. Two men shall be in the field; the one shall be taken, and the other left." And they answered and said unto Him, "Where, Lord?" And He said unto them, "Wheresoever the body is, thither will the eagles be gathered together."""

And then the words of John I began to speak and declare unto this people, for in this day shall the end draw nigh and nation shall gather themselves together to defeat the children of God, and the very powers of Satan shall be unleashed as never before seen by man. And I heard as it were the voice of a great multitude, and as the voice of many waters, and as the voice of mighty thunderings, saying, "Alleluia: for the Lord God omnipotent reigneth. Let us be glad and rejoice, and give honor to Him: for the marriage of the Lamb is come, and His wife hath made herself ready." And to her was granted that she should be arrayed in fine linen, clean and white: for the fine linen is the righteousness of saints. And he saith unto me, "Write, blessed are they which are called unto the marriage supper of the Lamb." And he saith unto me, "These are the true sayings of God." And I fell at his feet to worship him. And he said unto me, "See thou do it not: I am thy fellowservant, and of thy brethren that have the testimony of Jesus: worship God: for the testimony of Jesus is the spirit of prophecy. "

And I saw heaven opened, and behold a white horse; and He that sat upon him was called Faithful and True, and in righteousness He doth judge and make war. His eyes were as a flame of fire, and on His head were many crowns; and He had a name written, that no man knew, but He Himself. And He was clothed with a vesture dipped in blood: and His name is called The Word of God. And the armies which were in heaven followed Him upon white horses, clothed in fine linen, white and clean. And out of His mouth goeth a sharp sword, that with it He should smite the nations: and He shall rule hem with a rod of iron: and He treadeth the winepress of the fierceness and wrath of Almighty God. And He hath on His vesture and on His thigh a name written, KING OF KINGS, AND LORD OF LORDS.

And I saw an angel standing in the sun; and he cried with a loud voice, saying to all the fowls that fly in the midst of heaven, "Come and gather yourselves together unto the supper of the great God; that ye may eat the flesh of kings, and the flesh of captains, and the flesh of mighty men, and the flesh of horses, and of them that sit on them, and the flesh of all men, both free and bond, both small and great." And I saw the beast, and the kings of the earth, and their armies, gathered together to make war against Him that sat on the horse, and against His army. And the beast was taken, and with him the false prophet that wrought miracles before him, with which he deceived them that had received the mark of the beast, and them that worshipped his image. These both were cast alive into a lake of fire burning with brimstone. And the remnant were slain with the sword of Him that sat upon the horse, which sword proceeded out of His mouth: and all the fowls were filled with their flesh.

And I saw an angel come down from heaven, having the key of the bottomless pit and a great chain in his hand. And he laid hold on the dragon, that old serpent, which is the devil, and bound him a thousand years, and cast him into the bottomless pit, and shut him up, and set a seal upon him, that he should deceive the nations no more, till the thousand years should be fulfilled: and after that he must be loosed a little season. And I saw thrones, and they sat upon them, and judgment was given unto them: and I saw the souls of them that were beheaded for the witness of Jesus, and for the Word of God, and which had not worshipped the beast, neither his image, neither had received his mark upon their foreheads, or in their hands; and they lived and reigned with Christ a thousand years. But the rest of the dead lived not again until the thousand years were finished. This is the first resurrection.

Blessed and holy is he that hath part in the first resurrection: on such the second death hath no power, but they shall be priests of God and of Christ, and shall reign with Him a thousand years. And when the thousand years are expired, Satan shall be loosed out of his prison, and shall go out to deceive the nations which are in the four quarters of the earth, Gog and Magog, to gather them together to battle: the number of whom is as the sand of the sea. And they went up on the breadth of the earth, and compassed the camp of the saints about, and the beloved city: and fire came down from God out of heaven, and devoured them.

And the devil that deceived them was cast into the lake of fire and brimstone, where the beast and the false prophet are, and shall be tormented day and night for ever and ever. And I saw a great white throne, and Him that sat on it, from whose face the earth and the heaven fled away; and there was found no place for them. And I saw the dead, small and great, stand before God; and the books were opened: and another book was opened, which is the Book of Life: and the dead were judged out of those things which were written in the books, according to their works. And the sea gave up the dead which were in it; and death and hell delivered up the dead which were in them: and they were judged every man according to their works. And death and hell were cast into the lake of fire. This is the second death. And whosoever was not found written in the Book of Life was cast into the lake of fire.

And I saw a new heaven and a new earth: for the first heaven and the first earth were passed away; and there was no more sea. And I John saw the holy city, new Jerusalem, coming down from God out of Heaven, prepared as a bride adorned for her husband. And I heard a great voice out of heaven saying, "Behold, the tabernacle of God is with men, and He will dwell with them, and they shall be His people, and God Himself shall be with them, and be their God. And God shall wipe away all tears from their eyes; and there shall be no more death, neither sorrow, nor crying, neither shall there be any more pain: for the former things are passed away."

And He that sat upon the throne said, "Behold, I make all things new." And He said unto me, "Write: for these words are true and faithful." And He said unto me, "It is done. I am Alpha and Omega, the Beginning and the End. I will give unto him that is athirst of the fountain of the water of life freely. He that overcometh shall inherit all things; and I will be his God, and he shall be My son. But the fearful, and unbelieving, and the abominable, and murderers, and whoremongers, and sorcerers, and idolaters, and all liars, shall have their part in the lake which burneth with fire and brimstone: which is the second death."

And there came unto me one of the seven angels which had the seven vials full of the seven last plagues, and talked with me, saying, "Come hither, I will show thee the bride, the Lamb's wife." And he carried me away in the spirit to a great and high mountain, and showed me that great city, the holy Jerusalem, descending out of Heaven from God, having the glory of God: and her light was like unto a stone most precious, even like a jasper stone, clear as crystal; and had a wall great and high, and had twelve gates, and at the gates twelve angels, and names written thereon, which are the names of the twelve tribes of the children of Israel: On the east three gates; on the north three gates; on the south three gates; and on the west three gates. And the wall of the city had twelve foundations, and in them the names of the twelve apostles of the Lamb.

And he that talked with me had a golden reed to measure the city, and the gates thereof, and the wall thereof. And the city lieth foursquare, and the length is as large as the breadth: and he measured the city with the reed, twelve thousand furlongs. The length and the breadth and the height of it are equal. And he measured the wall thereof, an hundred and forty and four cubits, according to the measure of a man, that is, of the angel. And the building of the wall of it was of jasper: and the city was pure gold, like unto clear glass. And the foundations of the wall of the city were garnished with all manner of precious stones. The first foundation was jasper; the second, sapphire; the third, a chalcedony; the fourth, an emerald; the fifth, sardonyx; the sixth, sardius; the seventh, chrysolyte; the eighth, beryl; the ninth, a topaz; the tenth, a chrysoprasus; the eleventh, a jacinth; the twelfth, an amethyst. And the twelve gates were twelve pearls: every several gate was of one pearl: and the street of the city was pure gold, as it were transparent glass. And I saw no temple therein: for the Lord God Almighty and the Lamb are the temple of it.

And the city had no need of the sun, neither of the moon, to shine in it: for the glory of God did lighten it, and the Lamb is the light thereof. And the nations of them which are saved shall walk in the light of it: and the kings of the earth do bring their glory and honor into it. And the gates of it shall not be shut at all by day: for there shall be no night there. And they shall bring the glory and honor of the nations into it. And there shall in no wise enter into it any thing that defileth, neither whatsoever worketh abomination, or maketh a lie: but they which are written in the Lamb's Book of Life.

And he showed me a pure river of water of life, clear as crystal, proceeding out of the throne of God and of the Lamb. In the midst of the street of it, and on either side of the river, was there the tree of life, which bare twelve manner of fruits, and yielded her fruit every month: and the leaves of the tree were for the healing of the nations. And there shall be no more curse: but the throne of God and of the Lamb shall be in it; and His servants shall serve Him: And they shall see His face; and His name shall be in their foreheads. And there shall be no night there; and they need no candle, neither light of the sun; for the Lord God giveth them light: and they shall reign for ever and ever.

And he said unto me, "These sayings are faithful and true: and the Lord God of the holy prophets sent His angel to show unto His servants the things which must shortly be done. Behold, I come quickly: blessed is he that keepeth the sayings of the prophecy of this book." And I John saw these things, and heard them. And when I had heard and seen, I fell down to worship before the feet of the angel which showed me these things. Then saith he unto me, "See thou do it not: for I am thy fellowservant, and of thy brethren the prophets, and of them which keep the sayings of this book: worship God." And he saith unto me, "Seal not the sayings of the prophecy of this book: for the time is at hand. He that is unjust, let him be unjust still: and he which is filthy, let him be filthy still: and he that is righteous, let him be righteous still: and he that is holy, let him be holy still. And, behold, I come quickly; and my reward is with Me, to give every man according as his work shall be. "

"I am Alpha and Omega, the Beginning and the End, the First and the Last. Blessed are they that do His commandments, that they may have right to the tree of life, and may enter in through the gates into the city. For without are dogs, and sorcerers, and whoremongers, and murderers, and idolaters, and whosoever loveth and maketh a lie. I Jesus have sent Mine angel to testify unto you these things in the churches. I am the Root and the Offspring of David, and the Bright and Morning Star. And the Spirit and the bride say, 'Come.' And let him that heareth say, 'Come.' And let him that is athirst come. And whosoever will, let him take the water of life freely. "

For I testify unto every man that heareth the words of the prophecy of this book, if any man shall add unto these things, God shall add unto him the plagues that are written in this book: And if any man shall take away from the words of the book of this prophecy, God shall take away his part out of the Book of Life, and out of the holy city, and from the things which are written in this book. He which testifieth these things saith, "Surely I come quickly." Amen. Even so, come, Lord Jesus. The grace of our Lord Jesus Christ be with you all. Amen.

7 THE WICKED ONE

It was sunrise on Easter Sunday when the spirit of the Lord spoke to me concerning the many nations which had risen in power, nations that had ruled over the world, nations that conquered and destroyed other nations, nations that were mighty and militant, nations that one thought would never be destroyed because of their great power and riches.

After the Spirit of God had spoken to me about the space of an hour, a great sleep came over me. I the Prophet of the Lord do testify of the things which the Lord showed me in my sleep. For the Lord did command me to write down all things He would show me in my dream. In obedience to God I wrote down all that I saw. For the Lord did show me great and mighty things.

Behold the heavens were opened, and I saw a great city that shined even as the sun. The city was majestic in all its color and array. Angels ascended and descended upon this great city. The city was so majestic and bright that it radiated its beauty and splendor as far as the eye could see. Suddenly, I realized I was beholding the City of God with mine own eyes. For surely this was the Kingdom City that the Majesty on High did rule from. Its splendor was so beautiful that I felt faint beholding its beauty.

In that great city did go forth angels of God. Angels that ascended and descended upon the great city. The angels were incredible and their beauty was great. The angels moved with swiftness as they carried out the decrees of our Lord. Their swiftness was great, and each moved upon the command that was given to them with great haste. Their number was great and each did go forth accordingly as they were commanded. The streets of the city appeared busy. Streets were filled with angels and they did travel back and forth throughout the city. Each angel moved in manner of their direction with great swiftness.

Suddenly an angel appeared and said unto me, "What seekest thou?" I said unto him, "I know not. For the Lord did speak unto me the space of an hour and behold a sleep came upon me, and lo, I have found myself in this great city and knowest not whither to go." The angel then said unto me, "Follow, I have something to show thee." He then took me by the hand and I was then standing in the midst of this great city, and when I had noticed angels all around me, I was driven to my knees because of the presence and holiness of the Lord Almighty.

Then the angel knelt and said unto me, "Rise and behold the temple of God." Suddenly strength returned unto me. I rose to my feet and behold, I saw the Lord sitting upon a throne, high and lifted up, and his train filled the temple. Above it stood the seraphim: each one had six wings; with two wings he covered his face, and with two wings he covered his feet, and with two wings he did fly. And one cried unto another, and said, "Holy, holy, holy, is the Lord of Hosts: the whole earth is full of His glory." And the posts of the door moved at the voice of him that cried, and the house was filled with smoke. For there the Glory of the Lord did shine and go forth.

I then said, "Woe is me! for I am undone; because I am a man of unclean lips: for mine eyes have seen the King, the Lord of Hosts, now I will surly die." Then the angel said unto me, "Thou will surely not die for the Lord has shown you this great thing." I looked, and the temple was great and did shine with reflection of the glory of the Living God. I suddenly noticed that through the brightness there was smoke that filled the temple all about. As I inhaled the smoke, it was like fire going through my body. As I breathed I felt faint as the glory of God did fill my soul.

Suddenly I heard the voice of the Lord, saying, "Whom shall I send, and who will go for Us?" For some reason I felt boldness and courage and I cried, "Here am I; send me." And the Lord said, "Go, and tell My people all that I shall show and tell thee. Go, tell thy people that they may clearly see with their eyes and hear with their ears. For this day I will show thee a thing that no man hast seen. Ye shall hear the foundation of heaven shake. Ye shall see the stars of heaven fall. Fear ye not, for thou shall be numbered among My people," saith the Lord, "and no harm shall come unto thee."

After the Lord had spoken to me I felt very weak. Then my body fell to the floor of the temple and I awoke again in the same place that I had fallen, but there were different angels about me. As I searched for the angel that had brought me to the temple, another angel lifted me up from the floor and said unto me, "Who art thou?" Remembering that I was not to be afraid, I said unto him, "I am a servant of the Most High." Then the angel took me from inside the temple and brought me to a place I knew not. It looked much like the earth and the angels there were singing and did give praise to the Living God.

The place I stood was glorious to behold: beautiful trees, and every imaginable color in the flowers that bloomed. The sky was bright and clear. Everything seemed to glow. I noticed a beautiful stream that flowed with sparkling water. In front of me was a hill where there was gathered a multitude of people. I beheld what seemed to be a worship service. I noticed that there was one angel that stood out from the rest. He was beautifully adorned and did shine as the sun. His robe was majestic, and his beauty was breathtaking. His garments were sown together with precious jewels, and He stood upon a hill, leading the praise in song. I looked and beheld that the music which was too great to describe did come from within this angel. He sounded himself like the orchestra, and all the angels did marvel at his greatness for he was great to behold. As he played and sounded his instruments, his beauty did go forth by reflection of his garments.

The songs they sang did lift up the Living God and they where sung in such manner that the sound seemed to come from everywhere. Even the ground we stood upon seemed to give praise to the Lord. My heart was filled with gladness and joy at the worship and praise for it was a song that I had never known. For the song seemed to have power and strength. With each note there was a holy awareness of God's holiness. Suddenly, I noticed as I stood gazing at the congregation, the words of the song went forth out of my own mouth. It was a song I knew not, but the words did fill my mouth, and my heart did burn with adoration for the Living God.

Suddenly the music stopped and I only heard Lucifer, the angel of the Lord, begin to speak unto the congregation. I heard him for a moment, and mine ears were sealed up that I could no longer hear again. As fear started to come over me, I remembered what the Lord had said unto me and my countenance did strengthen again.

As the congregation stood listening to the Angel of the Lord, I looked and behold, the heavens above started to slowly dim till there was little light. I could see the angels waving their hands toward Lucifer and continually the place I stood darkened until the garments of luster failed to radiate the beauty that I saw at the start. Then an angel grabbed my hand and immediately I was back in the temple of God.

Suddenly, I found myself standing in the back of the temple. As I looked there I saw the angel of the Lord that led in music standing at the front of the congregation. His beauty had failed him, and he stood before the throne of God. Then I heard a voice that did shake the temple, and it was the voice the Majesty on High. Then the Lord said unto Lucifer, "This day shall I drive thee and thy servants out from the temple. I have prepared a place for thee in the center of the earth. There thou shalt be bound for eternity, and shalt burn all thy days, but this shall I do at the Judgment. For now, shalt I drive thee from My presence; ye and thy servants shall be eternally cut off from this place."

"Thou art judged this day because thou hast said in thine heart, "I will ascend into heaven, I will exalt my throne above the stars of God: I will sit also upon the mount of the congregation, in the sides of the North." Why hast pride filled thine heart? Every precious stone was thy covering, the sardius, the topaz, and the diamond, the beryl, the onyx, and the jasper, the sapphire, the emerald, and the carbuncle, and gold. The workmanship of thy tabrets and of thy pipes was prepared in thee in the day that thou wast created. Thou art the anointed cherub that covereth; and I have set thee so: thou wast upon the holy mountain of God; thou hast walked up and down in the midst of the stones of fire."

"Thou wast perfect in thy ways from the day that thou wast created, until iniquity was found in thee. By the multitude of thy merchandise they have filled the midst of thee with violence, and thou hast sinned: therefore I will cast thee as profane out of the mountain of God: and I will destroy thee, O covering cherub, from the midst of the stones of fire. Thine heart was lifted up because of thy beauty. Thou hast corrupted thy wisdom by reason of thy brightness. I will cast thee to the ground. I will lay thee before kings, that they may behold thee."

Then when the Lord had finished sentencing Lucifer, the Lord said unto him, "Thou shalt be called Satan, because thou art an enemy unto Me and My creation. Thou art Mine adversary this day. I beheld Satan as lightning fall from heaven, and the heavens shook as he was driven out, and sin and iniquity was driven out, and it caused a great sound to come forth out of the heavens, a sound that is heard unto this day."

After these things I awoke and did write all that I saw, and all that the Lord told me that day, for the things that the Lord showed me was great. For that day I saw Satan judged and sentenced for the iniquity that he did commit against the Lord. And I numbered those that were cast out with him that day to be one third of the Heavenly Host. For the number was great, and great was their fall that day before the Lord.

And I beheld the face of the angels of the Lord, those that were cast out and those that remained committed to the service of the Lord Almighty. For the countenance of them that fell before their iniquity was one of beauty and a wonder to behold, but iniquity did strip them of their beauty, and I saw their appearance change as they were cast out, and it was the countenance of a wild beast because of the sin that filled them.

Then the Lord said unto me, "Write the things down which I, the Lord, shall tell thee concerning this matter, for today great mysteries shall be known unto thee." Then the Lord began to tell me of great things I knew not, nor should I have understood except by revelation from God. And I, the servant of the Lord, did take and write down all that the Lord did tell me, for great is the Lord and His Word.

And the Lord God said, "Let Us make man in Our image, after Our likeness: and let them have dominion over the fish of the sea, and over the fowl of the air, and over the cattle, and over all the earth, and over every creeping thing that creepeth upon the earth." So God created man in His own image, in the image of God created He him; male and female created He them. And God blessed them, and God said unto them, "Be fruitful, and multiply, and replenish the earth, and subdue it: and have dominion over the fish of the sea, and over the fowl of the air, and over every living thing that moveth upon the earth."

And God said, "Behold, I have given you every herb bearing seed, which is upon the face of all the earth, and every tree, in the which is the fruit of a tree yielding seed; to you it shall be for meat. And to every beast of the earth, and to every fowl of the air, and to every thing that creepeth upon the earth, wherein there is life, I have given every green herb for meat:" and it was so. And God saw every thing that He had made, and, behold, it was very good, and thus were those words recorded in the Scripture.

From the day that man was created, the Lord breathed into his nostrils and made him a living soul. And the Lord God took the man, and put him into the garden of Eden to dress it and to keep it. And the Lord commanded the man, saying, "Of every tree of the garden thou mayest freely eat: but of the Tree of the Knowledge of Good and Evil, thou shalt not eat of it: for in the day that thou eatest thereof thou shalt surely die." And the Lord said, "It is not good that the man should be alone; I will make him an help meet for him." And out of the ground the Lord formed every beast of the field, and every fowl of the air; and brought them unto Adam to see what he would call them: and whatsoever Adam called every living creature, that was the name thereof. And Adam gave names to all cattle, and to the fowl of the air, and to every beast of the field; but for Adam there was not found an help meet for him.

And the Lord caused a deep sleep to fall upon Adam, and he slept: and the Lord took one of his ribs, and closed up the flesh instead thereof; And the rib, which the Lord had taken from man, made He a woman, and brought her unto the man. And Adam called his wife Eve, for she was the mother of all living. And Satan beheld the Lord's creation and said in his heart, "I will destroy God's creation. I will so corrupt man that he shall serve me instead of the Lord. I will rule over him and cause his days to be short. I will search and tempt man to lure him into all manner of wickedness, therefore causing the Lord to judge man for all his sins." Immediately Satan and his servants conspired ways to deceive God's creation and destroy them that day.

Then Satan said to himself, "I will ally with the woman, for she is the weaker vessel, and I will destroy this race of people," and Satan used a serpent to carry about his will. Now the serpent was more subtle than any beast of the field which the Lord God had made. And he said unto the woman, "Yea, hath God said, 'Ye shall not eat of every tree of the garden?'" And the woman said unto the serpent, "We may eat of the fruit of the trees of the garden: but of the fruit of the tree which is in the midst of the garden, God hath said, 'Ye shall not eat of it, neither shall ye touch it, lest ye die.'"

And the serpent said unto the woman, "Ye shall not surely die: for God doth know that in the day ye eat thereof, then your eyes shall be opened, and ye shall be as gods, knowing good and evil." And when the woman saw that the tree was good for food, and that it was pleasant to the eyes, and a tree to be desired to make one wise, she took of the fruit thereof, and did eat, and gave also unto her husband with her; and he did eat.

There God beheld what Satan had done and how he deceived the woman and caused the man to sin, and God said to Satan, "I will put enmity between woman and thee for she was deceived and she shall not ally with you." The Lord said, "I will greatly multiply thy sorrow and thy conception; in sorrow thou shalt bring forth children; and thy desire shall be to thy husband, and he shall rule over thee." And unto Adam He said, "Because thou hast hearkened unto the voice of thy wife, and hast eaten of the tree, of which I commanded thee, saying, thou shalt not eat of it: cursed is the ground for thy sake; in sorrow shalt thou eat of it all the days of thy life; thorns also and thistles shall it bring forth to thee; and thou shalt eat the herb of the field; in the sweat of thy face shalt thou eat bread, till thou return unto the ground; for out of it wast thou taken: for dust thou art, and unto dust shalt thou return. "

Unto Adam also and to his wife did the Lord make coats of skins, and clothed them. And the Lord said, "Behold, the man is become as one of Us, to know good and evil: and now, lest he put forth his hand, and take also of the Tree of Life, and eat, and live forever:" Therefore the Lord sent him forth from the garden of Eden, to till the ground from whence he was taken and it was that day that the Lord required blood to cover man's sins and to hide his nakedness. So He drove out the man; and He placed at the east of the Garden of Eden cherubim, and a flaming sword which turned every way, to keep the way of the Tree of Life.

Then Satan, when he saw that his plans had failed, his anger and greed against God was kindled the worse, and he fought the harder, for he hated God and now hated mankind. For he knew that God loved His creation and it pleased His heart to make mankind.

And Satan did send forth his servants everyone according to their rank into the earth and there prepared to destroy man. And there were aligned ranks that did go forth from the earth even into the heavens. For there was much hate and anger kindled against mankind, and Satan said, "I will war against God's people till I have destroyed every man and made God a fool before His creation."

And Satan formed powers and ranks and placed them both on earth and in the heavens, for Satan knew that unlike God, he could not be but one place at a time. He knew that he must counterfeit the chain of command that God did place in order with his servants. And Satan named these orders principalities, powers, rulers of the darkness, and spiritual wickedness. And such would be the elements of evil that man would wrestle with until the end.

Of the spirits, some were given domain upon the earth. Some were assigned task to perform, and in time the spirit world did strategically align themselves against the earth and God's creation to destroy it. Some of the servants of Satan were placed to corrupt nations and others to pollute cultures. Others were ordered to afflict God's children, while others were to strengthen the perversion of mankind on the earth. Each had their place and each knew and gave an account for all they did against man. Thus every demon took their place against the will of God, even unto this day.

And the strength of this force was great, and it was so that God's servants wrestled against these powers, for the sake of man, that God's will to be done. And the Word records, "Yet Michael the archangel, when contending with the devil he disputed about the body of Moses, durst not bring against him a railing accusation, but said, 'The Lord rebuke thee. "'

In all the powers that Satan brought forth against God's people, he also appointed powers to corrupt the mind of man. He chose servants to bring every form of wickedness to mind, so that man might destroy himself. But God stood against Satan and always had a willing servant that would uphold what was holy and righteous. No matter what happened and how angry God was with His creation, there was a servant that would come through. From time past when God destroyed the earth with water, there was one that would say no to the devil and yes to the will of God.

And it came to pass, when men began to multiply on the face of the earth, and daughters were born unto them, that the sons of God saw the daughters of men that they were fair; and they took them wives of all which they chose. And the Lord said, "My Spirit shall not always strive with man, for that he also is flesh: yet his days shall be an hundred and twenty years." There were giants in the earth in those days; and also after that, when the sons of God came in unto the daughters of men, and they bare children to them, the same became mighty men which were of old, men of renown.

And God saw that the wickedness of man was great in the earth, and that every imagination of the thoughts of his heart was only evil continually. And it repented the Lord that he had made man on the earth, and it grieved him at his heart. And the Lord said, "I will destroy man whom I have created from the face of the earth; both man, and beast, and the creeping thing, and the fowls of the air; for it repenteth me that I have made them," but Noah found grace in the eyes of the Lord.

After these things Satan did come against man again to build a tower to reach the heavens. Continually, Satan sought out to destroy man in some way, but God gave victory over and over again. And again the forces of Hell sought out a way to corrupt

God's people, and the whole earth was of one language, and of one speech. And it came to pass, as they journeyed from the east, that they found a plain in the land of Shinar; and they dwelt there. And they said one to another, "Go to, let us make brick, and burn them thoroughly." And they had brick for stone, and slime had they for mortar. And they said, "Go to, let us build us a city and a tower, whose top may reach unto heaven; and let us make us a name, lest we be scattered abroad upon the face of the whole earth."

And the Lord came down to see the city and the tower, which the children of men builded. And the Lord said, "Behold, the people is one, and they have all one language; and this they begin to do: and now nothing will be restrained from them, which they have imagined to do. Go to, let us go down, and there confound their language, that they may not understand one anther's speech." So the Lord scattered them abroad from thence upon the face of all the earth: and they left off to build the city. Therefore is the name of it called Babel; because the Lord did there confound the language of all the earth: and from thence did the Lord scatter them abroad upon the face of all the earth.

Then God began to use the forces of evil to chastise His children, because God realized the power of sin and how the afflictions of the devil were great, and they would cause men to turn unto Him rather than remain in sin. For sin, when it is finished, bringeth forth death and the hunger of sin is never quenched till man has nowhere else for deliverance accept for the mercy of God.

And after Satan and his forces began to grow in number over the earth, God raised up nations to chastise His children, that they would walk holy before Him and refuse to serve the devil, for God did judge nations with nations and because of the sins of Israel, God did allow nations to chastise them. And what Satan meant for corruption and insult, God used for His glory in the carrying out of judgment for the sins of His people.

69

Then the Lord showed me in another vision a great thing. I looked and I did see the council of wickedness that did set themselves against nations, and I looked, and as nations would rise and nations would fall, the council reigned over them. Each great nation would fall into the hands of Satan, and his demons would seek the same will for each nation from times past until this day.

In each nation there have remained the same powers to see its rise and its fall. For the fall of a nation was known only to man, but the will of Satan remained the same, and that will was carried out. For Satan was no respecter of nations nor their governments, but the sin and destruction was his concern. And these powers that sought after these nations went from one to the other, only to destroy man and God's holiness, but through all, the Lord has remained faithful to His children. For Satan has failed to realize that the governments rest upon the shoulders of the Almighty. Though nations rise and nations fall, the will of God is carried out by His children and His servants. For only mankind studieth the rise and fall, but God knoweth all things. And His will shall be done in earth as well as in heaven.

There I saw also in that vision the forces of evil aligning themselves against God's children, against even the Jew. For the Jew has wondered the face of the earth being driven out from one city to the other and so forth. For the council that caused their first affliction was the same that, in time, would lead them into the fire, the death chambers, and the torture of nations to the north.

Even as the church began to build after the death and resurrection of the Son of God, Satan followed the church and everywhere did deceive and bring persecution. For in times past Satan aligned himself with the great church which did persecute the Christians and all those that believed. He caused nations to rise against nations, villages against villages, that the Christian who protested the sins and corruption of this world would be slain and burned alive. Man and woman alike were tortured for protesting the idolatry and sin of the great whore church. For blood was shed for much time as Satan deceived and led fights against the child of God. And in all manner that man did act, was and is to the fulfilling of evil against God.

For Satan united the great perversions and doctrines of fallen nations and did pervert the Word of God and cause one great religion to come forth that he could use to control and abolish the Gospel. For though this great church did war against the truth, and against God's children, in time the true church was strengthened and overcame. And in all that Satan did to destroy the church, it was strengthened by that very vice.

As I saw the persecution of God's people, I saw the familiar presence of evil. In each nation did the wickedness of Satan go forth and all was instigated by the same, for these servants of Satan have been commanded this thing, and it is their mission and their passion even unto the rise of that man of sin that is soon to come.

8 THE UNBORN CRY

One day when I was praying, the Spirit of the Lord spoke to me and commanded me to number the children of this nation. When I asked the Lord for what purpose should I do this great thing, again He said, "Arise, go ye and number the children of this nation. I shall return unto thee not many days to inquire of thee." So after prayer, I did as the Lord commanded that I may please Him. For days I searched and numbered the children and when I finished, the Lord returned unto me to inquire of my finding.

And the Lord said unto me, "Hast thou did according to My command?" I said unto the Lord, "I have." "Ye have numbered the children which escape the hand of death, but what is this that I do hear in Mine own ears? I hear the children crying out to Me even while they are yet in the womb. What is this that I hear, and this that I see? For I see children which cannot be numbered by man lying in the pits, their bodies torn like the lion teareth its prey. Even the stench of death doth stretch itself into the heavens."

When I heard what the Lord said unto me, I was ashamed and fell unto the ground and wept bitterly. My heart was sore, for I feared the wrath of God upon this nation. I knew that the Lord would prevail against such wickedness in haste, and judgement was sure to follow. I thought unto myself, "What have I done to stop this wickedness against the children of this nation?" Then the Lord, knowing my thoughts, said unto me, "Arise and strengthen thyself. Many have chosen to hide this evil from themselves. Ye have thought well concerning this matter, only it is too late to save all the children. My people could have prevailed against such evil in the day that it was found to be wicked by My church. Now, many justify this hideous act of brutality not only in the schools, but in My house as well."

Is it not written, "And they brought young children to Him, that He should touch them: and His disciples rebuked those that brought them. But when Jesus saw it, he was much displeased, and said unto them, 'Suffer the little children to come unto Me, and forbid them not: for of such is the Kingdom of God. Verily I say unto you, whosoever shall not receive the Kingdom of God as a little child, he shall not enter therein.' And He took them up in His arms, put His hands upon them, and blessed them."

"Did I, the Lord, not make man above the animals of the earth? And now they are brought low, even unto the place of the wild beast and thrown into the trash pit for the fowl and the worm to eat. Who hast numbered the dead among the trash heaps of the earth, for the stench of their corps doth fill the air, for they are many?"

"Is there a famine in the land that goeth forth to destroy the children? Is there a famine that can discern the wanted and unwanted children of our land? For I have numbered the children this day, and a multitude doth sleep in the grave. Know ye this day that the sting of death hast not been kindled against these, My children? I am a just God, what pleasure would I have in destroying the life I give? What manner of justice would I receive taking the breath away from a child that I have created? For this is no sickness nor pestilence, but rather is the hand of death that goeth out to destroy Our youth."

"For the blood of these children doth run in the streets and their voices are heard. I see their beautiful faces, for they are quickly come unto Me. Did I not command, 'Thou shalt not kill?' And these, My children, are taken even from the womb of the mother. Is not the physician come but to help the sick that they may escape the arms of death, and now by their hands that I have directed in wisdom and knowledge, are the children slain? Is there one that can stop this murder?"

"Ye say unto yourselves, even as the wicked sayeth, 'These children are not yet alive in their mother's womb, but only art a piece of flesh.' Nay, they are a living soul that I have given life to. Have ye not read, 'And it came to pass, that, when Elisabeth heard the salutation of Mary, the babe leaped in her womb; and Elisabeth was filled with the Holy Ghost: And she spake out with a loud voice, and said, "Blessed art thou among women, and blessed is the fruit of thy womb." And ye men that are counted wise among your peers and this nation, doth rise up and declare for the child that it is not, howbeit, My Word declares otherwise.'"

"Arise, go ye out and declare My Word. I have called thee out to speak against this iniquity. Stand ye up this day and declare My Word to this generation. Why hast thou murdered such children that cannot speak in defense? What wrong have they done to deserve such judgment? I have weighed them in the balance and found them innocent. They have committed no sin. They have not transgressed My laws. Ye have judged them unfairly, for they art innocent and have not the ability to speak for themselves, but I the Lord shall speak for them. Their cries are made from the womb. Can ye not hear their cry when the tool is come in unto them like the sword? For they cry with the pain of a man as they are ripped apart out of their mother's womb. Who has played the part of the death angel? For I am the Lord, I give, and I require a man's life."

"Thy hands are stained with the blood of children. Ye shall not hide from Me, for in that day that ye are brought before Me, ye shall see the blood of children on your hands and it shall be red like crimson that day. Thy countenance shall change and ye shall cry out that day, for ye will know the truth. It will be too late to wash thyself of this wickedness. Your sin shall find you out on the judgment day. Know ye this day, only the blood of Jesus shall wash away thy sins. Today, if ye will call upon the name of Jesus Christ, His blood shall cleanse thee even now. Many shall stand before the throne of God with the blood of children dripping from their hands. Who shall save them in that day?"

"I have heard the innocent cry of the children, and because they have no defense, I will fight for them, yea, I will fight for them this day. I will stand in and be their judge. I hear, and I see there faces, for they are now come unto Me. Ye murderers, why hast thou done unto the children this horrible thing? Their cry is silenced to your ears, but I hear their screams of pain. Ye generation of murderers, why hast thou brought this sin upon yourselves? Why have ye judged the children for the transgressions of the mother and the father? I say again, I the Lord will be their defense and their judge at the appointed time."

"O mother, ye that bring life from thy womb into this world, why hast thou slain thy child? Today it is expedient that ye pray that ye may see the fruit of thy womb. My anger is kindled against thee this day. Repent, for thou hast done wickedly in the sight of the Lord. Pray that ye may see the fruit of thy womb, for they doth fill the heavens with their presence. And now thou art childless and cannot feel their tenderness, ye have said in thine heart, 'It is not convenient that I be found with a child.' Thou hast said in thine heart, 'I will not deliver my child and teach it the ways of the Lord. I will sacrifice my child to the goddess Ashtoreth.'"

"Ye foolish and wicked men, why dost thou choose to curse the soul of your child? I have heard thy plea to the mother to have thy seed murdered. Do ye think for one moment that the murder of thy son or daughter shall hide thy iniquity? Woman, have ye chosen to pluck out the fruit of thy womb to cover thine iniquity? What sin hast thy child committed against thee? Why hast thou allowed the instruments of death to take life from thy seed? For in this sin thou hast rejected My Word. Thou hast rejected My commandments and ye shall be judged for thy wickedness."

"Ye have worshipped other gods. For I am one God, a jealous God indeed, and ye have turned your backs to Me and went whoring after the gods of this world. Ye have sacrificed thy purity unto the god of the Zidonians. Thou hast revealed thy nackedness and hath brought shame and corruption to thy flesh. Ye have have sinned a great sin against thyself, and who shall save thee in the end? Shall Ashtoreth deliver you from My hands on Judgment Day? Even she will turn her back on thee in that day. O ye wicked generation, not only do ye sacrifice thyself unto the gods of this world, but ye have torn thy seed from the mother's womb and laid it down on the altars of thy idols."

"Where are the fathers of the unborn? Where is he that doth lay with the woman to cause such sin to be revealed? Ye may say in thy heart, 'We will slay the child and bring forth life at another time.' Why dost thou chose to send thy woman to a house of slaughter than to grant life to thy seed? Are ye a coward, and ye choose to hide thy sin from others? Thou hast even tried to hide thy sin from Me. Know ye not that I am the Lord and I knowest all things, both in heaven and on earth, and ye think of Me as ye think of the fool. Dost thou set thy face against Me and defy My Word? I have seen the proud look on thy face and the corruption in thy heart. Thy sin hast numbered thee among the fools. Repent and turn to me, for I shall save thee from the wrath to come."

"Ye doctors that do this wickedness, ye shall surely be judged for thy sin. Thy punishment shall be greater than the mother. Put down thy instruments, and turn from thy wickedness this day. The cries of the children are heard as ye fill their bodies with the water like unto the waters of the Dead Sea. Even in their mother's womb doth the child attempt to flee from thy sword, but where shall he hide, for I have placed the child near the mother's heart to be protected from all danger. Is their an escape for the unborn from this death? Yea, this day I call every man that would take up sword against a child to repent. "

"I, the Lord, am merciful and I will yet forgive this sin. Repent, and turn unto Me, I will be thy God and ye shall be My people. Is it too late? Nay, I will forgive thee and save thee from that dreaded Day of the Lord. Why hast thou not heeded My servants that have went before me to expose this great sin? Ye have cursed them and locked them away in your prisons. I have sent prophets to declare My Word and thou hast turned thy ear away from them. Great are their rewards, for they have done my will. And now this nation has brought forth laws that they may not protest this murder."

"Satan, thou has worked hard to bring wickedness into the hearts of this nation, but I am the Lord and do make my salvation known to this nation. And in Me they shall have eternal life forever. And you lieth to them and many believe your word, but ye are close to the end. Thou shalt be bound up in chains and cast into the pit forever."

9 THE UNKNOWN BEAST

It was during the spring of the year, when the Word of the Lord came to me concerning a great wickedness in the land, a wickedness that devours like the lion but is friendly like unto a lamb. And the Lord said unto me, "Get thee up and tell this, My Word, to thy people that they may repent of their sins and escape My judgment. For I am the Lord and I will give My Word unto thee this day." And I, the prophet of the Lord, did remember all that the Lord spoke unto me, and I declare it unto this nation.

"Ye rulers of this great nation, thou sayest in thy speeches that you do this or that for the people. Yet I do hear the people cry out to Me, saying, "Deliver us from this wickedness that has come to us." Ye have burdened thy nation down with many taxes. Ye have lied to thy people and hast blamed thy wickedness on every person other than yourselves. Ye spend that which is not yours to spend and demand that which is not yours for the taking. With every dollar there is a lie to justify thy craftiness."

"Why hast the homes of this land been invaded by thy hand? Have I not chosen the head of every household, and yet ye have rejected My Word and have sought out ways to bring thy nation into bondage. Your heart is filled with sin because ye have meddled into the business of many, destroying that which is right before the Lord. Even My church has stood quietly, like a sheep to the slaughter, concerning this wickedness. On the outside your intentions seem to be good, but on the inside ye have sought to destroy the families."

"I created every living thing that exists on the face of this earth, and I have set in motion My laws which shall not fail. Ye have said in thy heart, 'The God of heaven is not one that should take care of His own,' but rather ye have proposed government programs to do the work that I freely give and have promised. Thy heart has become bitter toward Me this day because ye have strayed from My statutes and have bowed down to the gods of this world. Ye have made idols to bow thyself down to. Ye say that the Lord hath turned a death ear to His own, but this day let it be known that God is not a man, that He should lie; neither the son of man, that He should repent: hath He said, and shall He not do it? or hath He spoken, and shall He not make it good?"

"I say unto you this day, I know thy heart and I know what thou hast said and murmured unto thyself. For it is written, 'I have been young, and now am old; yet have I not seen the righteous forsaken, nor his seed begging bread.' Ye have turned your backs unto Me for the things of this world and I am a jealous God. Ye will not serve two masters. Look at thyself, consider thy gods today. What peace hath they given to you this day? What liberty is found in thy heart? Your gold hath bound your hands and feet like chains. What liberty is found in serving your gods? Ye walk tall filled with pride at day, but ye are given over to fear in the night. Who can deliver you from this curse?"

"Many have been deceived by the ways of this world, choosing to listen to the reasoning of fools than to stand on the promises of the Living God. Ye have sought out ways to care for the world, only to care for thy own wickedness. Your father, the devil, knoweth that in the day that ye believe in the one True and Living God, even I Am, you will be given a sound mind and transformed into a new creature. My treasure shall be thy treasure, My kingdom shall I share with thee. Ye shall even be as My child and an heir to My bounty. Be not deceived this day by the babbling of fools. They know not the things concerning the promises of God, but rather they have created an antichrist system to withstand the trial of life."

"This nation, like so many, hath said unto themselves, 'We will supply the needs of thy inhabitance. We shall feed the hungry, we shall clothe the naked, and we shall shelter the homeless.' Are not these things supplied and freely given to the children of the Lord? Thy gratitude is laced with poison and deceit for thy people, ye care not for their lives. Ye care only to look good before men, that ye may obtain favors to quench your lust. Ye care not for the widow, but that your name may be lifted up before men. Doeth thou these good deeds in private? Nay, ye give so that ye may obtain, and be seen by man."

"Thy goods and perverted kindness have I called the church to attend. It is the duty of My children to look out after the poor and widowed. It is the place of the church to care for the one that is without. I have called out My people to hearken to the needs of the people, but I see many needs go unmet before the world. My providence is a testimony to the world that I am God, and I shall provide for My own. But where is he that is ready to go out into the world to deliver My Word?"

"Did not the Son of Man feed those that were hungry as He taught the Words of Life? Where are the deacons that are to minister to the church? Have they set themselves up to rule and be filled with arrogance against such needs that the Son of Man gave himself for? I shall reward thy deeds openly before the earth in time; seek not to be lifted up before man."

"I have even searched the heart of many that are called to minister the Word and pastor over the churches scattered abroad. Some have said to themselves, "The poor offereth nothing to the church. They have not a contribution to the church, nor unto people. The afflicted are a sore sight among the church of God. The prisons are no place to harvest souls that the attendance may increase, what money shall they bring into the church? The children hath nothing to offer, they too have become a hindrance to progress."

"Some hath said in their hearts, 'I will water down the truth that I may entertain the rich, the publican, even the heathen. I will hide from them sound doctrine that I might obtain favor and even gifts from the world.' Many churches have transformed themselves into places for social events, choosing rather to ignore My commandments. My sanctuary has become a place to gamble, to drink, and a place to mock even My name."

"I have called My people out to be light unto the whole world and a refuge to those that are heavy burdened. Today, I shall deliver My people from such vanity if they will call upon the name of the Lord. I will heal them and forgive their sins. I will cast their sins from My presence, never to be remembered again. Repent, for the Kingdom of God draweth nigh. Save yourselves while it is day, for the hour cometh when no man shall be delivered from My judgment."

"And as for the heathen that goeth about to deceive the world, even My own, I knoweth thy craftiness. Thy secrets are revealed this day before thee and thy neighbor. Your ways are foolish and bringeth death, not life unto thy people. Thy ways of mercy shall be a stumbling block before this generation. Thy show of kindness shall be a noose and shall drain this nation from its wealth, even unto collapse."

"Money is your god and ye shall, in the end, be poisoned by its sting. All ye that have set out to do good for this nation shall be brought down low. Thy ways shall be a hindrance to growth and vanity shall be the end thereof. Shall thy hunger for riches ever be quenched? I know thy ways this day. Ye say, 'I will tax all persons, and they shall bring their offering before the nation, and it shall be a balm before the whole world.' Thy promises to the inhabitance of this land are all lies. Ye tax unfairly and never deliver that which is promised in thy great speeches. The voices of this nation cry out unto thee to deliver them from such burden. This day let it be known unto all, blood and tears are not to be paid as taxes unto this nation."

"Ye nation of robbers and murderers, how long will thou continue to commit this great sin against thy people and unto the Lord? Ye care not for the people of this land. A man's sin cannot be taxed and expected to bless. A man's blood cannot be required for a tax. Yet thou art blind to this great wickedness in the land. Do ye think that everyone will play the part of a fool? Ye cannot cover this sin from me, for I am the Lord. Thy hearts are blackened with greed and lust. Ye hide the truth from thy people because ye are like unto your father, the devil. Thinkest thou that thou can build this nation with the blood and tears of thy inhabitance? O ye fools, ye sacrifice thy nation to the beast that ye may prosper in wealth. Ye hath not the truth, yet ye would judge men, as one that is fair and honest. The truth is hid far from thee because thou hatest me and hath not known the truth."

Then, I, the servant of the Lord, did see a vision. In the vision was a great beast like creature having two faces. Only one face could be seen of man at a time. Suddenly there was the sound of what seemed to be millions of voices crying. I said unto myself, "What is this that I see, and this that I do hear? I hear mourning throughout all the land. A mourning for the child that is now dead. I hear the cry of children for their mother and their father. I hear the mother crying out for her husband, yet he is dead, even in the grave. "

"Is there a famine in the land that killeth the people of this great nation? I see the dead that cannot be numbered. This famine is great, and it destroys like a beast. It has no respect for anyone, young or old. Is there not one that can save this land? Where are the leaders of this nation? I see them, but they sit quietly in the gates turning their heads away from the people."

"Ye rulers and governors of this nation, can ye not see the corpses as they stack up in the streets? Can ye not hear thy people as they mourn the dead and art fearful for themselves? Even thy kinsmen have ye turned a deaf ear to. Has thy heart become as the stones? Are ye hardened to the cry of thy own mother and father? Thy greed will judge thee at the appointed time. I knowest thy heart and it is filled with iniquity. It is set on serving the mammon of this earth. Ye search out to gain power over thy own, and betray them behind their back. This day shall it be declared unto all the land that the beast which thou hast fattened shall destroy you and tear your flesh to shreds before thee and thy own people, for they shall see judgment come against thee."

Then I saw in a vision a great beast, one which consumed the flesh of this nation, yet appeared to do many wonderful things in the sight of men. The beast which I saw had two faces; one was like unto that of a lamb, the other I could not see because of its swiftness to keep hid. The lamb face of the beast did great things in the sight of the people and kept its head turned where no one could see its hind parts. And the lamb appeared to be kind and gentle to all that were in its presence.

The appearance of the lamb was clean and beautifully adorn by men. The lamb sat in high places and did go about, seemingly to do good. The lamb was welcomed in many places; from the church to the great city that ruleth over this nation. It was a friend to all, and did go in and out of each home that it was welcomed. The lamb was made rich by both the rich and the poor. It was kind to the weak as well as the strong. Then I noticed that the feet of the beast were many, so great in number I could not count.

I said to the Lord, "This is a good thing, and the people doth make progress because of the beast. How is this thing come unto me? I heard the voices of sorrow in the vision, yet it is the same beast. The lamb beast is fattened by many and doth appear to be kind to all manner of persons. How can this be, for I heard voices crying out and yet I heard nothing from the lamb but the praises of all men, both small and great?" Then I prayed unto the Lord that I might see the other head of the beast. Surely, it is one that should be adorned and loved as well.

Then the Lord said unto me, "This beast is no friend to man, but is the work of the devil, for it worketh wickedness both day and night. It showeth its pretty side and withholds its back to all. This beast is quick to kill any that will come against it. Even My people that are called by My name are deceived by its good works. This beast is ever present with each generation, but these people, even this nation, have fattened the best and made it strong. The beast will never be destroyed by man, it holds this nation in ransom, and there is none that can deliver man from this beast. Only I can destroy the beast and save man from its claws."

"There was a time that this nation did rise up against this beast, but it was not fattened like it is now. I saw men as they took the beast and bound it and they did cut the head off. They left the beast alone and it lay wounded for a time. Its feet did remain and gave unto the beast strength. For the beast is given strength by its feet instead of its head. Even its feet were greatly wounded, but with time, the beast did heal. Now that the beast is healed, it is stronger than it has ever been and is hungry for the blood of its people."

I said unto the Lord, "Show me this beast that I may see its hinder parts. I will see the other head for myself that I may understand what Thou sayest." Then the Lord took me behind the beast and showed me this great sight. My heart fell as I looked upon its face. As I beheld this beast my body grew weak and I fell to the earth and did mourn for what I saw. I cried out unto the Lord because my heart was heavy. I then slowly managed to help myself up that I could see more of this vicious beast. Though my strength was gone out of me, I saw again the beast.

Suddenly a great stench filled the air, such as I had never smelt. It was the smell of flesh that lay everywhere I did look. Behold, there were people of every walk that did mourn for the dead. There was a great mourning, one that seemed to be a constant wail. I looked and behold, I saw the beast. It was like a great dragon, and it kept its head turned in such a way that no one could see the other side of its body. The dragon was great and fierce, and did eat the flesh and drink the blood of all that was in the path of the lamb. The beast was covered in the blood of its prey; it was so covered with blood that it appeared red and smelled like a corpse. The great dragon did follow behind the lamb and went wherever the lamb led it.

I looked and behold, dead men's bones did appear everywhere. Bones that could not be numbered for there were many. Some of the dead where starved to death and others were crushed and dismembered. The dragon had no mercy on whomever it preyed. There were the bodies of the great men and poor men. I saw the parts of the mothers as they lay slain beside their young. I wept. I thought to myself, "This is surely the work of the devil, and the people are blind." Then I heard the dragon give a fierce cry and it shook itself as it devoured a man, ripping him apart with his claws.

I then turned and I saw a woman who was holding a child in her arms. Her face was down over the child as she wept bitterly while stroking the child's hair. The woman looked up at me and stared as she held the child out for me to see. Her face was bruised and her clothes were rent. Her countenance was filled with bitter grief. As for the child, I could see it was a little girl and she lay dead in her mother's arms. I then asked the woman, "Where is thy husband?" Then the woman lowered her head and did weep all the worse.

As I continued down the street, I came across a garden that was filled with beautiful trees and flowers. I could hear birds singing, and the squirrels did leap from tree to tree. I thought to myself, "The beast has not found this place," for its beauty was great.

And lo, I saw a man sleeping upon the ground and I walked over to him and would have talked with him for a time, but he was weak and could not move. I looked and his eyes were as dead men's eyes. His clothes were torn, and he smelled like unto the beast of the field. His head lay in vomit and it stank. He lay there helpless and there was nothing I could do.

I realized the beast was one beast with two heads, but there seemed to be two worlds. I then heard the mourning of a family and did hurry that I might see this cause. I looked and behold, there lay a young man in the street with his brothers and sisters and both parents leaning upon his neck. The family called out to the Lord and did bitterly weep. I said to myself, "This is surely a child of the Living God," and, "Why is he destroyed by this beast? What wrong has he done to deserve such a thing?" Then the Lord said unto me, "He that liest dead has done nothing wrong, but he was a victim of another man's sin. For the beast neither regards the child of the Living God from the wicked." As I looked upon this great tragedy, I wept bitterly with the family and did comfort them in their grief.

After a while I continued walking. Suddenly, I saw a great multitude of people standing in the midst of the dead. There faces were even as the faces of them that lay below. They seemed to be bound in chains awaiting for a judgment of some kind. I wept for them because there ears where sealed up and they could not hear. There were young and old alike in the crowd, and their number was so great they could not be counted. As one would fall from the crowd dead, two would take their place. I said to the Lord, "Is there not an end to this number?" The Lord answered not.

As I traveled on there were homes that lined the street, and I could hear the screaming of many. Each house seemed to be different in a sense, yet the footprints of the beast did mark the ground. I could see children hiding under the house in fear of their lives as the men bitterly beat the mothers, yet I could do nothing but look. Parents were arguing and screaming at one another. I could hear both men and women swearing and cursing one another as they fought against each other. My heart did go out to these children, but there was nothing I could do.

I then saw a woman sitting on the porch of her home weeping as she sat and stared at the ground. I looked and there lay a knife that was covered in blood. Then she heard my coming and she was afraid. I said to her, "Look at me," and she slowly lifted her head. Her face was scarred and there were many bruises. Most of her scars were healed over, but left their print. I then removed the coat from around her and saw her battered and bruised body. Tears flowed from her as I looked upon her back. She was ashamed and did hide her face from me, for she had been greatly tormented.

I asked her, "Who did this horrible thing to you?" The woman just cried the louder. I was compelled for some reason to go into her house. As I opened the door I was astonished at such a site. The house was destroyed inside with broken things all around. The walls were cracked and stained with blood. As I turned in the hall I could see bottles setting all around and I smelled the scent of wine. Then I looked down and there lay her husband on the floor.

There was a weapon beside the man's hands, and he lay dead, his body yet warm. I got on my knees and rolled him over to see what had killed this man. There I saw where he had been stabbed in the heart. And on the floor, blood and wine did mix. Then the vision left me, and I remembered all that I saw.

I then said to the Lord, "This vision is great and it troubleth me sorely. What shall I say, for this thing is great and needeth to be interpreted." Then the Lord said unto me, "The beast is the beast of addiction. He doth make himself a friend and devoureth his prey like a lion. Thy nation hath fattened this beast and it goeth about wherever it will. It is a beast of the vineyard and of the herbs and medicines of man."

"The beast doth make this nation fat. Its drink is taxed with a great tax, and because of the greediness of this nation and its rulers, they use this beast to build and to do great works. They think in their hearts that they can control the beast, but it is too late. No one can see both sides of this beast unless he discerns well the things of the Lord and for this reason this nation will continue to be deceived."

"The beast studieth corruption and has its mark on much wickedness that is found in this nation. Even My people are deceived by its voice. It sayest good things and maketh promises to all, but death and destruction follows behind wherever it goeth. This nation is given over to its cruelty and there is no hope for its death. The homes are where men doth drink until well drunk, or they partake of the herbs of the field, they beat their wives, and doth abuse their children."

"Men and women inject its poison into themselves, hoping to escape the pains of life. But they are bewitched by many that would claim to have wisdom. They inhale the smoke of herbs and medicines, hoping to escape, but only for a short season. Their misery is multiplied by such wickedness and yet, it is often their misery that brings such anger against society. They seek to escape from the responsibilities of life, but what they run from is the conviction of the Lord. The wickedness of their heart is revealed unto them. They seek to escape the reaping of their own lust. They know not that their lust shall consume them unto death. They hear not My servants, but mock as the nation joins with them and their foolishness. How long shall they continue to lie to themselves?"

"This nation has hardened its heart and refuseth to hear and see with their own eyes. Families are destroyed in the path of one drunkard, and yet we try to separate the lamb from the dragon. For I the Lord doth declare it is one beast. A beast filled with blasphemy against me. The beast doth spew poison that men say is a medicine to the body. The poison is consumed and doth hide guilt and pain, but the poison is quickly turned into a great serpent that striketh out and killeth all that is around. The bite of the serpent does not always bring sudden death but killeth its victim slowly."

Then the Lord told me to write and declare His Word to the people of this nation. For it is written in the proverbs, "Wine is a mocker, strong drink is raging: and whosoever is deceived thereby is not wise. For the drunkard and the glutton shall come to poverty: and drowsiness shall clothe a man with rags. As a thorn goeth up into the hand of a drunkard, so is a parable in the mouth of fools."

"In this nation, I have set my scales against thee that I might judge thee for thy transgression. Thou hast done evil in My sight and turned what was evil from the start to good. Be not deceived, I, the Lord, am not mocked. I shall pour out my wrath against this people for they have destroyed this nation through their own greediness. The ways of this world are not the ways of the Lord."

"I have seen the poverty that lieth in the footprints of this beast. Its fury has been felt in all parts of the world and now my anger is kindled against such wickedness. Homes are broken, and lives torn apart by their loved ones. Because of this great sin, husband is turned against his wife, and wife against her own husband. Children who art innocent become trapped in this pit of wickedness."

"I hear the cry of the mother who is childless because of this great sin. For the dead doth cry out against this sin and yet are they silenced. Ye mean well in your doing, but sin can never be made righteous in my sight. I am the Lord and am holy; this thing is wicked and shalt be judged. Even now My judgment is poured out among men. Who can provide for this nation the paths of wisdom? For the one that giveth wisdom is yet ready and willing to offer all things according to God's riches to all men."

"The children do weep for they have been beaten sorely by their parents. They cry out in their tenderness unto me, and I the Lord heareth them. There are bodies afflicted with disease and starvation. This beast doth make thy mother and thy father rage against their own children. Ye nation of fools, can ye not see what thou doest? Ye doth destroy yourselves from the inside out. Ye are not capable of saving this nation from its fate, because ye are full of sin and hath become a slave to the addictions of the flesh. Thy soul doth lust after that which is wicked before the Lord. Thy wisdom is become the ration of a fool. "

"I smell the stench of dead men, and I shall look for their judge. Who hath appointed them unto death? Repent, o ye nation; thou hast sinned against the Lord. All that thou hast done with the money from the beast, it shall be brought down low. I shall tear down thy highways and all that thou hast built. Know ye not that I command the earthquake? And did I not separate the sea for My servant Moses to pass through on dry ground? For what shall stop the sea from raging against its shores and flowing into its coast? Did I not calm the sea and wind in the Sea of Galilee? For surely at my command I shall judge and tear down all that man has built. Even in the end it shall be burned up; only the soul that cries out unto Me in repentance shall I preserve and deliver in time of destruction."

"Thy schools shall not prosper from this beast, because it is sin. Sin shall never be rewarded, nether on this earth nor in heaven. Ye think that thou art wiser than the Lord? I say nay, but your wisdom is foolishness. How could ye do such wickedness and think ye could get away with it? Is it not written, 'It is appointed unto men once to die, but after this the judgment.' Ye shall not escape. Run for the corners of the earth. Dig thyself a cave and see if ye can hide from Me. I shall find thee, and in that day I shall laugh at thy destruction."

"Repent and turn from thy wickedness, for I shall save thee, and in the end I shall slay the beast that feeds off the blood of men and children. Surely the beast shall be judged in heaven, for in every man's heart lies the beast. For by the works of the flesh is the beast fed and enlarged. Ye only have power to slay the beast within through the blood of Jesus Christ."

"Ye wicked men, thy wisdom is counted among the dunghill, for thou hast said in thine heart, 'I shall escape the wrath of God.' Thy wisdom is brought low, even unto foolishness. Ye have fattened the beast with thine own sins and watched it devour your people, yet thou continue to turn thy head from the truth. If ye will seek truth, it shall set you free this day."

"Turn from thy wicked ways and hearken unto the voice of the Lord, for I am the Lord of Hosts, it is by My Word and My Spirit that ye can be delivered from the beast, lest ye fall prey unto it. This day I shall deliver thee from the hands of the beast. I can heal your soul and bring peace into thy home. God is not a man, that He should lie; neither the son of man, that He should repent: hath He said, and shall He not do it? or hath He spoken, and shall He not make it good?"

"Trust in the Lord this day for the salvation of thy soul and the deliverance of thy house from the bonds of sin. Repent ye backsliders from thy unfaithful ways, for the Lord is merciful and shall forgive thee of thy sins. Confess your transgressions and see the Lord raise you up even this day. Confess thy sins and behold the wounds of the beast as they are healed."

10 THE PERVERTED

Early in the evening the Word of the Lord came to me concerning wicked perversions in our land. And the Lord said, "Go and prophesy all that I shall tell thee. I, the Lord, doth search out the streets of thy nation and I have seen a great perversion among thy people. A sin that is against thy people, a sin that shall curse the rich and poor, the strong and weak. Even the perversion that was found in Sodom and Gomorrah in the days of Abraham My servant, is now found in thy people's heart and in thy streets. This sin doth defile even the command I gave man in the Garden. This people I have made in My image and saith unto them to be fruitful and multiply, they now sin against me and my command. For this sin is great and is now increased above many nations."

"Is there one that would cry out to spare this people from destructions such as in the day of Sodom? Knowest thou not that it written, 'Then the Lord rained upon Sodom and upon Gomorrah brimstone and fire from the Lord out of heaven; and he overthrew those cities, and all the plain, and all the inhabitants of the cities, and that which grew upon the ground?' And this great nation is found to be perverted like great cites."

"Even thy rulers doth bring men into their home that they may know them, and such as they would have done the same unto My servants outside of Lot's house. Thy cities are vexed with a great curse because of this sin. And because such wickedness is found among thy rulers, it is made good by thy laws of this nation. Even they shall be mocked by the heathen in their day of affliction. But I say unto you, this sin shall be judged and condemned on earth and in heaven at the Day of Judgment. Surely the curse shall cause the flesh to be consumed by pestilence and much affliction, such that has never been seen."

"This nation is full of abominations, and it is a stench in My nostrils. For it is written, 'If a man also lie with mankind, as he lieth with a woman, both of them have committed an abomination: they shall surely be put to death; their blood shall be upon them.' And now hath this sin been brought to My attention in this day. For such doth eat you up as leprosy, even a sickness that shall surely rob you of your life for it is unto death. Yet you curse Me and go about in your sin with a proud heart. I am the Lord, and I shall surely bring you low. I shall take you to the grave, then ye shall lift thine eyes in hell and cry out."

"I shall deliver thee if thou will cry out in repentance and turn from thy wicked ways. Today is the day of salvation. Save thyself while it is still day, save thyself while thy strength abides, for My judgment is at hand. And lo, now thy streets have filled with people that lie with their own kind, for a name is given unto thee: a gay, a lesbian, and thou art homosexual because thy liest with thy own kind; woman with woman, man with man; such is sin and will not stand in the Day of Judgment. For the soul that sinneth shalt surely die."

"Thy cities are filled with the perverted. They cry out to Me in curses. They swear concerning My judgments. Ye people are blinded and cursed because thou canst not replenish the earth. Ye are proud of your ways. Ye seek that ye may turn others over to this filthiness. Woe be unto you. Ye shall surly be brought down even to hell. Repent, and draw nigh unto Me this day; I shall heal thee and thy house this day; today is the day of salvation. There is none other that shall deliver thy soul from hell."

"Thou hast gained favor among the lawmakers, and some of them have turned unto your perversion. Thy laws are not to be fastened after such manner of sin, for in the day thereof it shall bring this nation low. I am the Lord Almighty, and I shall judge thee on this matter; even now My judgment is poured out. Yet thou art blind and deceived; ye have scales on your eyes. How long shall it take thee to awake and see the destruction at hand? Thou hast lied and made thyself a fool before others. Repent, and turn unto Me, for I shall protect thee in time of judgment. For as much as I have breathed life into man and made him a living soul, I have been forced by the sin of this world to cast thee into a place prepared for the wicked one, even Hell that is enlarged. "

"And now, this sin has been proclaimed to thy merchants and has brought a reproach in the workplace, yet thy laws are fashioned in this day to protect such filthiness. For there is a natural division that rest between people who would seek to defile themselves with such perverseness and those who would not. And yet thou hast even made laws to enforce this offense of mankind. Why hast thou done such things in the sight of the Lord? Is not this land yet free? Is there one that would stand in defiance, or would you silence him in your prisons? Why hast thou written laws to protect such perversion? What business do they have dealing with this matter? What is one sin for another, for all sin shall be judged in the end."

"Even thy military is now filled with such abomination that they cry out. Such corruption shall spread in the camps and bring strong men's hearts down. They cry for the shame of such, but what can be done? The morale is low and it shall be a stumbling block to this nation in time of war. For a man of war should be strong and mighty, not weak in mind and turned over to the ways of a woman. For these people seek occasion to sin against themselves and others. Their mind is corrupt and they seek corruption wherever they go. Their ways are not natural as to that of a man and woman, but are perverse. I have made the animals of the field to behave in such manner above that of this wicked sin. Have ye become lower than the animals of the earth that I have given thee dominion over?"

"Ye think in thy heart that ye have answers to all the questions, but I say nay, because thou hast committed this sin and justified it in thine heart, thy mind is made that of a fool. Why dost thou seek to destroy others with your sin? Is it not satisfied? Is your lust not quenched with your own kind, or will you try to rob every man and every woman of their virtue and nature? Ye even seek after the children of your people, that ye may uncover the nakedness of a child. I shalt surely destroy you. For I have heard the cries of My children, and whosoever shall offend one of these little ones which believe in Me, it were better for him that a millstone were hanged about his neck, and that he were drowned in the depth of the sea."

"Ye have filled the schools with thy perversion, seeking to indoctrinate these little ones. Ye seek after the lust of the flesh and thy flesh shall be consumed in fire for thy transgressions. Because of thy favor with rulers, ye have found a place to do thy craftiness. They protect thee in their courts, but who shall protect you when the Day of Judgment is at hand? Who shall deliver thee out of mine hands? Even Satan your father shalt be bound in chains forever in the pit."

"Save yourself while there is still day. For Satan seeketh after your soul; he is no friend of man, but an enemy to all. For Satan, the thief, cometh not, but for to steal, and to kill, and to destroy: I am come that they might have life, and that they might have it more abundantly. Repent, for the hour cometh when no man shall be delivered from My hands, for soon time shall be no more and I shall judge every man according to his deeds. In that Day of Judgment ye shall be thrown into the fire of hell where there is weeping and gnashing of teeth."

11 THE PLAN OF SALVATION

From this point on, the things written herein are real and based upon the Word of God. I hope that your life has been inspired up to this point. It is urgent to deal with a few questions before continuing in this chapter.

Did you find yourself falling victim to the judgments of God?

Did you find yourself in the category of the mislead, the wicked, the fool, or the sinner?

Did you know that if you are not a child of God, you will some day stand before a holy God and give an account for your life? In fact, if you are not a Christian and have never confessed Christ as your Savior, there is coming a day that in heaven you will bow your knees and confess with your mouth that He, Jesus Christ, is Lord. I would invite you to confess Him now. You will save yourself a lot of grief in the future. The fact of the matter is that by confessing him now as Lord, and believing in your heart, you will receive eternal life and escape the eternal torment of the flames of Hell. If you wait until you stand before God in heaven to confess Him, it will have been too late.

Let me ask you a question right now. If you died this very moment, would you go to Heaven? Are you absolutely sure you would die and enter into Heaven and live in the presence of God for eternity? Did you know that you can be sure this day where you will spend eternity? If you are not sure where you will go when you die, my friend, it is very unfortunate, according to the Word of God, you would spend eternity separated from God and burning in a devil's Hell. Now I know that no man would wish this upon himself, but you have reached a point of decision. If you ignore this plea for accepting Christ as Savior, you have decided to reject Him. Don't fall victim to procrastination. There will be many that will find themselves waiting till it is too late to make a decision about their destiny.

Today, I invite you to make that decision. You can finally, once and for all, know that you have eternal life. Will you say, "Yes, I want to accept Christ as my Savior. I want to serve God, and have my sins forgiven. I want assurance this day in my heart. I want peace in my life, my home, and in my heart." The good news is, in just minutes, you could know beyond a shadow of a doubt that you will be saved for eternity and brought into fellowship with God.

I would like to share with you how you too can experience life-changing salvation. You may ask the relevant questions, "But why do I need to be saved? What did I do?" The reason is very simple, my friend. In the beginning when God made man, he put them in the garden and told them to multiply, and they were pure before God. However, there was one command that God gave man in the garden. (Gen 2:16-17) *"And the LORD God commanded the man, saying, Of every tree of the garden thou mayest freely eat: But of the tree of the knowledge of good and evil, thou shalt not eat of it: for in the day that thou eatest thereof thou shalt surely die."*

It wasn't long until man disobeyed God and ate of the forbidden tree, and because of God's Word, man had to die. But death is not like you and I see it in the natural; death is also spiritual. Because of the sin of one man, God cursed them both and drove

Adam and Eve out of the garden and out of His presence. From that time on man has been born living outside the presence of God. Because of the nature of sin and the curse of God on Adam that day, sin was forever passed down through the blood of every person born thereafter, and God, being holy, could not look upon sin. Therefore, man fell out of fellowship with God. (Rom 5:12) *"Wherefore, as by one man sin entered into the world, and death by sin; and so death passed upon all men, for that all have sinned."*

Friend, that's only the beginning of the story. You see, God loved man. He loved man so much that, according to the Bible, He would visit with Adam and Eve in the cool of the day. Can you imagine the Lord wanting to walk with you each day as well? Did you know that He wants to walk with you? In fact, He is willing to put your past behind Him and not only walk with you, but live inside of you. The problem is, since you are a sinner you have been sentenced to death, and, therefore, you are separated from God. Did you know that everyone has sinned and everyone has been sentenced to death? (Rom 3:23) *"For all have sinned, and come short of the glory of God."*

Of all the people that have lived on the face of this earth since Adam, there has never been a person naturally born outside of sin. There has never been but One that could stand before God declaring Himself righteous and without sin. No matter how good you are, you are not good enough before a righteous God. The Bible declares: (Rom 3:10) *"There is none righteous, no, not one."* *(Isaiah 64:6) "But we are all as an unclean thing, and all our righteousnesses are as filthy rags."* So you see, friend, it is nothing personal against you and what you might have done; it is a matter of our sinful condition in the presence of a holy God.

Yes, friend, there is no hope for mankind trying to save himself, for his fate is death. Some believe that if they live right and do good deeds they will make it to heaven eventually, but good deeds will not save you. The Bible says, (Eph 2:8-9) *"For by grace are ye saved through faith; and that not of yourselves: it is the gift of God:*

Not of works, lest any man should boast." You see, there are plenty of people that are good folks and live a very productive, charitable life; but they are also sinners in need of a Redeemer.

There is one way to be sure that you can go to heaven. There is one way that you can be acquitted from the sentence against you. There is One that can save you if you will put your trust in Him—that person is Jesus Christ. Jesus said (John 14:6) *"I am the way, the truth, and the life: no man cometh unto the Father, but by Me."* Friend, there is a price to pay for being a sinner. Sin has a cost, and the cost is the death and separation of mankind from God forever. (Rom 6:23) *"For the wages of sin is death…"* But today God has a special gift for you because He goes on to say in that verse *"…but the gift of God is eternal life through Jesus Christ our Lord."*

(John 3:16-18) "For God so loved the world, that He gave His only begotten Son, that whosoever believeth in Him should not perish, but have everlasting life. {17} For God sent not His Son into the world to condemn the world; but that the world through Him might be saved. {18} He that believeth on Him is not condemned: but he that believeth not is condemned already, because he hath not believed in the name of the only begotten Son of God." (John 20:31) "But these are written, that ye might believe that Jesus is the Christ, the Son of God; and that believing ye might have life through His name."

My friend, you can be forgiven from all your past and start all over again. All the sin you have ever committed can be wiped clean. (Isaiah 1:18) *"Come now, and let us reason together, saith the LORD: though your sins be as scarlet, they shall be as white as snow; though they be red like crimson, they shall be as wool."* Isn't that great news today? (Mat 11:28) *"Come unto Me, all ye that labour and are heavy laden, and I will give you rest."* Aren't you tired of running? I know that you could use some rest. How would you like some real peace? *(Phil 4:7) " And the peace of God, which passeth all understanding, shall keep your hearts and minds through Christ Jesus."*

Today you must die for your sins. You must die to that old nature and let God resurrect your life. What you need is to trust in the Lord Jesus Christ for your Salvation that you may be born again. (John 3:7) *"Marvel not that I said unto thee, 'Ye must be born again.'"* (John 3:3) *"Jesus answered and said unto him, 'Verily, verily, I say unto thee, Except a man be born again, he cannot see the kingdom of God.'"* You see, when you accept Jesus Christ as your Savior, you become a new person. (2 Corinthians 5:17) *"Therefore if any man be in Christ, he is a new creature: old things are passed away; behold, all things are become new."*

Jesus has already paid your debt. God sent His only Son to this earth to live and die and be a sacrifice for your sins and mine. In order for God to give life back to man, a life had to be sacrificed. Someone had to love you and I enough to give their life for us to live. (Rom 5:8) *"But God commendeth his love toward us, in that, while we were yet sinners, Christ died for us."* He not only died for us, but He took on our sins that we could be free unto righteousness. (1 Pet 2:24) *"Who His own self bare our sins in His own body on the tree, that we, being dead to sins, should live unto righteousness: by whose stripes ye were healed."*

The question you may be asking yourself is, "What must I do to be saved?" (Acts 16:30-31) *"And brought them out, and said, 'Sirs, what must I do to be saved?' {31} And they said, 'Believe on the Lord Jesus Christ, and thou shalt be saved, and thy house.'"* The Bible says (2 Corinthians 6:2) *"For he saith, I have heard thee in a time accepted, and in the day of salvation have I succoured thee: behold, now is the accepted time; behold, now is the day of salvation."*

Are you ready to believe that Jesus Christ is the Son of God and that He died for your sins? Today is the day for you to surrender your life to the will of God. The Lord is ready for you to trust Him for eternal life. (Rev 3:20) *"Behold, I stand at the door, and knock: if any man hear My voice, and open the door, I will come in to him, and will sup with him, and he with Me."* If you are ready, I want you to pray this prayer right now.

"Lord, I do believe that Jesus Christ died for my sins. I am a sinner, and I repent of all my sins. I want to walk according to Your will from this day forward. Thank You for sending Your Son to die for me on the cross. I accept by faith that His blood has cleansed me of all my sins. Lord, I also thank You for the righteousness that You have imparted unto me this day for trusting in Jesus Christ as my Savior. Help me be Christ-like in all that I do. Help me grow in wisdom and knowledge. Help me understand Your Word, and help me to let my light shine before all men. I ask all these things in Jesus Christ's name, Amen."

My friend, welcome to the family of God. At this moment, rest assured that you are saved and justified before God. You can now enter in before God and have full fellowship with Him. In fact, you are not the same person that you were a while ago. You see, now you have received the Holy Spirit; He has taken up residency in your heart. Yes, you have a part of God living in you right now. If you will submit to God, the Holy Spirit will lead you in all truth. You can hold your head up high because now there is no condemnation against you. (Rom 8:1-2) *"There is therefore now no condemnation to them which are in Christ Jesus, who walk not after the flesh, but after the Spirit. For the law of the Spirit of life in Christ Jesus hath made me free from the law of sin and death."*

If you accepted Jesus Christ as your Savior, I would like to hear from you. If you would, write to me and share how God has changed your life. If this book has inspired you through its message of repentance and commitment to the spreading of the Gospel I would like to hear from you as well.

Never in the history of this nation has the urgency for the Gospel been so great than this hour. With the church in the state that it is in due to the influence of this world, revival is needed in the heart and lives of every believer.

If you committed your life to Jesus Christ in response to this book, or if you have questions concerning this book, you may contact Melvin E. Barnett at melvin@melvinbarnett.com

ABOUT THE AUTHOR

Melvin Barnett has been ministering the Word of God since 1986. Today, the author enjoys life as a husband, father, and pastor. Through the years he has served in ministry under many titles. From working as a Chaplain in a substance abuse facility to serving as the Executive Producer of Christian television programs, he has been blessed to minister to a vast range of needs from people with various social backgrounds.

Melvin began ministering the Gospel at the age of seventeen. He has a Shepherd's heart and distinctly enjoys teaching the Bible, evangelism, and one-on-one encouragement through life coaching.

Website: www.melvinbarnett.com
Email: melvin@melvinbarnett.com